Invisible writing
and the Victorian novel

MANCHESTER
UNIVERSITY PRESS

For Shannon Russell

Invisible writing
and the Victorian novel
Readings in language and ideology

Patricia Ingham

Manchester University Press
Manchester and New York

distributed exclusively in the USA by St. Martin's Press

Published by Manchester University Press
Oxford Road, Manchester M13 9NR, UK
and Room 400, 175 Fifth Avenue, New York,
NY 10010, USA
http://www.manchesteruniversitypress.co.uk

Distributed exclusively in the USA by
St. Martin's Press, Inc., 175 Fifth Avenue, New York,
NY 10010, USA

Distributed exclusively in Canada by
UBC Press, University of British Columbia, 2029 West Mall,
Vancouver, BC, Canada V6T 1Z2

British Library Cataloguing-in-Publication Data
A catalogue record for this book is available from the British Library

Library of Congress Cataloging-in-Publication Data applied for

ISBN 0 7190 5201 7 *hardback*
ISBN 0 7190 5202 5 *paperback*

First published 2000

07 06 05 04 03 02 01 00   10 9 8 7 6 5 4 3 2 1

Designed and typeset
by Freelance Publishing Services, Brinscall, Lancs.
Printed in Great Britain
by Bell and Bain Ltd, Glasgow

Contents

	Acknowledgements	*vii*
	Note on quotations	*ix*
1	Invisible writing	1

Questions

| 2 | The question of *Vanity Fair* | 15 |

Tense

| 3 | Past and present in *The Mill on the Floss* | 39 |
| 4 | Gain and loss: the magic future in *Daniel Deronda* | 63 |

Deixis

| 5 | Who, when and what: deixis in *Bleak House* | 93 |

Negatives

| 6 | Maiden no more: negative values in *Tess of the d'Urbervilles* | 121 |
| 7 | Nobody's fault: the structural scope of the negative in *Little Dorrit* | 144 |

	Postscript	163
	References	165
	Index	171

Acknowledgements

I wish to thank in particular Jenny Harrington and Shannon Russell for their help in writing this book; and Penny Boumelha for reading and commenting on it. I am also indebted to David Smith, Alison Corley and Juliet Chadwick of St Anne's College Library; and to the News International Research Fund.

Note on quotations

Quotations from the novels discussed are taken from the following editions:

Vanity Fair, ed. J. Sutherland (Oxford: Oxford University Press, 1998)
The Mill on the Floss, ed. G. S. Haight (Oxford: Clarendon Press, 1980)
Daniel Deronda, ed. G. Handley (Oxford: Clarendon Press, 1984)
Bleak House, ed. N. Bradbury (Harmondsworth: Penguin, 1996)
Tess of the D'Urbervilles, eds J. Grindle and S. Gatrell (Oxford: Clarendon Press, 1983)
Little Dorrit, ed. J. Holloway (Harmondsworth: Penguin, 1985)

In these quotations, when emphasis is original to the novelist that is specified, otherwise emphasis is added by the author.

1

Invisible writing

THE purpose of the following chapters is to work on texts as heat works on 'invisible' or secret ink: by making visible aspects of writing normally unseen or unnoticed. In this way they counter treatments of language in literary works as largely a matter of vocabulary/lexis. The latter usually involves referring to words as 'signs', treating them as basic units and believing they are strung together like beads on a thread.

Such treatment results from the assumption that language as a system is linear in structure. In fact in any natural language sentences are structurally hierarchical. Their structure is best represented not by a line of words or signs added to each other as 'rich + old + men + women' but by the use of a tree diagram or mathematical bracketing which reveal their interrelationships. So the unit in question can be revealed as ambiguous, depending on who is rich and who is old. So it has three possible structures:

1 Rich old (men and women) i.e. both are rich and old
2 Rich (old men) and women i.e. only men are old but all are rich
3 (Rich old men) and women i.e. only men are old and rich.

It is at this level of hierarchical structure that much meaning is encoded. What the three analyses of 'rich old men and women' illustrates is the importance of scope or domain. The different meanings depend on deciding which of the nouns is referred to by the adjectives and which not. Similarly the logical category of negative scope refers to that part of the sentence that is covered by negation. Very similar sentences may have quite different meanings because of a difference in the scope of the negative. It may differ in very similar sentences or in some which are ambiguous. For instance the single sentence 'I didn't think he would do that' may be given two contrasting meanings which will be evident by the stress given in speech. It may be seen as negating the idea of having had a thought: 'It is not the case that I expected him to do that'. Or it may be read as 'I thought he would not do that'. Aspects of language involved in the structuring of sentences, what may be called its mechanics, are often ignored by those interpreting texts and by literary theories, although language itself is universally acknowledged to be central to both. This lack is capable of historical explanation and results in part from a recurrent but not altogether systematic exchange between language study and other disciplines involving a semiotic system.

Writing of 'semiology', 'a science which studies the role of signs as part of social life', Saussure's *Cours de linguistique générale* begins to draw parallels between language and other signalling codes: 'A language is a system of signs expressing ideas and hence comparable to … the deaf-and-dumb alphabet, symbolic rites, forms of politeness, military signals, and so on. It is simply the most important of such systems.' (Harris 1983:15). Saussure also risks a prediction: 'It is therefore possible to conceive of a science which studies the role of signs as part of social life … It would investigate the nature of signs and the laws governing them' (Harris 1983: 15). Though this science did not exist when the *Cours* was written, it 'has a right to a place ready for it in advance'. Saussure, however, sees linguistics as a subordinate discipline, 'only one branch of this general science' – semiology – which is the superordinate category (Harris 1983: 16).

This modest prediction has been more than fulfilled by the development of a semiotic approach to many areas from anthropology to fashion and boxing. But the relationship of language to what were expected to be merely other parallel disciplines has been more central than Saussure anticipated. Despite the theoretical defects of the structuralist accounts of language, its positive contributions to semiotic studies generally have remained unshaken. These contributions include the irrelevance to their meaning of the material nature of signs, the need to consider the signalling system as an interrelated set of units and the lack of transparency which requires its workings to be analytically decoded in order to understand them. Saussure's account of these ideas is sketchy and the material he uses to explain them is purely illustrative. He shows the irrelevance of the material nature of the sign by referring to the daily 8.45 a.m. train from Geneva to Paris. It may differ from one day to the next in all its material aspects – which engine, crew, carriages, passengers – but retain its identity. To make clear how language derives value from the interrelationship of units within its system, he compares it with chess: 'Consider a knight in chess. Is the piece by itself an element of the game? Certainly not. For as a material object separated from its square on the board and other conditions of play, it is of no significance for the player. It becomes a real concrete element only when it takes on or becomes identified with its value in the game' (Harris 1983: 107–9). In laying out his theory rather than producing an inductive argument, Saussure did not deal with sentence structure – he omitted to do so because he believed wrongly that sentence patterns were not part of a speaker's knowledge of the communal system but were part of an individual's linguistic creativity which allowed her or him to produce them in infinite variety (Harris 1983: 122). These are the foundations of semiology and the account of language in such terms is its key.

Since the early part of this century, linguistic terms and categories have become the *lingua franca* of semiotic studies including literary theory. A 'grammar' is seen as necessary for each discipline as well as a 'lexicon'. Language and its technical terms have become naturalized as the dominant tropes for semiotic analysis. It is unsurprising to read that 'Painting ... is a practice of representation and representation functions to transform and mediate the world through the specific *codes* it uses' (Nead 1988:8, my emphasis); or in a work on media semiotics that 'this chapter discusses film *signs* and *codes*, the central concern of semiotic analysis' (Bignell 1997: 174). In addition, as Frow points out, language is unique: 'Within the semiotic order language holds a privileged position in so far as the values generated in all other signifying systems can be translated into linguistic forms' (Frow 1986: 61–7).

Literary theory, like other disciplines, has drawn steadily for decades and usually belatedly on developments in linguistics to devise its own lexicon of terms such as *signs* (long discarded by linguists), *codes, discourse* and *competence*. In many cases the use of these terms is not literal but analogical. A simple example is *competence*, first used as a technical term by Chomsky for the 'ideal speaker-hearer's intrinsic competence' in his native language which Chomsky's grammar sets out to describe: 'We thus make a fundamental distinction between *competence* (the speaker-hearer's knowledge of his language) and *performance* (the actual use of language in a concrete situation)' (Chomsky 1965: 3). He explains that

> Linguistic theory is primarily concerned with an ideal speaker-listener, in a completely homogeneous speech-community, who knows its language perfectly and is unaffected by such grammatically irrelevant conditions as memory limitations, distractions, shifts of attention and interest, and errors (random or characteristic) in applying his knowledge of the language in actual performance. (Chomsky 1965: 4)

As Chomsky points out, conditions under which competence and performance coincide never exist: 'Only under the idealization set forth in the preceding paragraph [i.e. the previous quotation] is performance a direct reflection of competence. In actual fact, it obviously could not directly reflect competence'. For him competence is 'a mental reality' only (p. 4).

But as linguists concentrated more on what Chomsky called *performance*, the term began to be used differently in the phrase *communicative competence* with a sense relating easily to the normal use of the noun as 'acquired skill'. The literary theorist Jonathan Culler adopted the term to describe 'an implicit understanding of the operations of literary discourse which tells one what to look for'. Anyone without this knowledge,

> anyone wholly unacquainted with literature and unfamiliar with the conventions by which fictions are read would be unable to read it as literature – as we say with emphasis to those who would use literary works for other purposes – because he lacks the complex 'literary competence' which enables others to proceed. (Culler 1975: 114)

Culler's use has usually been accepted even by those disagreeing with his general argument.

Similar examples are found in the varying uses to which the term *code(s)* has been applied in literary theory. It is now used in sociolinguistics to refer to *code-switching* by speakers who control a repertoire of varieties of language, such as pidgin, regional or standard, appropriate to differing social situations. However, different literary theorists have analysed the 'codes' in literary works in different ways. Todorov defined them as *semantic*, *syntactic* and *verbal* but does not use these terms as linguists do to equate with 'meaning', 'sentence or phrasal patterns' and 'relating to a certain part of speech'. Similarly Roland Barthes in *S/Z* (1970) lists five codes: *proaretic*, *hermeneutic*, *semic*, *symbolic* and *referential*, with his own innovative definitions, using linguistic and other terms in a fairly arbitrary way.

In contrast, poststructualist accounts of language in the 1970s and 1980s are primarily philosophical, not linguistic, in their arguments. They move away from any exact description of the mechanics of language though they give it a privileged place in literary theory. Their interest focuses on a broad concept of 'the sign' (by this time no longer a technical term for linguists) in order to reconceive its nature and value. There seems to be a concern with the interrelationships in a linguistic system only in connection with a new analysis of the *signified* and the *signifier* (to use the usual translation of Saussure's terms for the two aspects of the sign). In stressing the importance of interrelationships between the units in a natural language system Saussure confined his detailed account to explaining how the two aspects of the sign fuse into a meaningful unit. He thought in phonological terms as the nineteenth century had learnt to grasp them: that differences of sound *perceived* by the native speaker constituted a mechanism for the construction of meaningful sound units. This involves ignoring differences between the variants of a single unit so that they are perceived as 'the same sound'. So for instance the sounds initially in *like*, finally in *cull* and after the initial consonant in *please* are all perceived as one sound 'l' (transcribed as /l/). The discernible sounds or phonemes transcribed as /l/ or /t/ and so on explain Saussure's statement that in the language system 'there are only differences' or contrasts (Harris 1983: 118). The nature of syntax and grammar is not within his remit. It is this area of what Saussure calls 'the signification and the signal [signified and signifier] considered *separately*' (Harris 1983: 118, my emphasis) that post-structuralists concern themselves with. Since Saussure does not deal with the combinations of words into meaningful structures, matters of syntax and grammar disappear.

A precise use of linguistic terms is made by those who practise 'stylistics' or 'linguistic criticism'. These methods are applied to short extracts from longer texts where the working of specific linguistic features can be examined. However, in mainstream theory and interpretation the broadly metaphorical use of linguistic terms prevails, often, though not always, with illuminating results. It is now generally accepted by authors who deal with social meanings and the nature and workings of ideology that language is a central issue to be addressed. Even Marx himself saw the exchange of commodities as a kind of language:

> by equating their different products to each other in exchange as values, they equate their different kinds of labour as human labour. They do this without being aware of it. Value, therefore, does not have its description branded on its forehead: it rather transforms every product into a social hieroglyphic. Later on, men tried to decipher the hieroglyphic, to get behind the secret of their own social product: for the characteristic which objects of utility have of being values is as much men's social product as is their language. (Mandel and Fowkes 1990: 166–7)

There have been differences among theorists as to how to position language in relation to ideology, itself a fluid concept. The extreme view is to see all ideology as a purely linguistic struggle. Michele Barrett, rejecting such a view, formulates the issue in question vividly: 'Are we really to see the Peterloo massacre, the storming of the Winter Palace in Petrograd, the Long March, the Grunwick picket – as the struggle of discourses?' (Barrett 1988: 95). Her implied answer seems to be 'surely not' – but certainly language embodies both social meaning and social action.

One exception to the theorists who ignore the mechanics of language is Bakhtin/Volosinov who, like Chomsky, had criticized the preoccupation of linguists with the sounds and forms (phonetics, phonemics and morphology). In a text published in Russian in 1929 he writes:

> Traditional principles and methods in linguistics do not provide grounds for a productive approach to problems of syntax ... All the fundamental categories of modern linguistic thought ... are thoroughly phonetic and morphological categories.

He rightly sees this as the result of nineteenth-century linguists' preoccupation with tracing family trees showing the interrelationships of Indo-European languages. He adds that 'such thought ... is incapable of viewing other phenomena of language except through the spectacles of phonetic and morphological forms. In consequence, the study of syntax is in a very bad state' (Matejka and Titunik 1986: 109). For Bakhtin, syntax or sentence patterns or the hierarchical structure of an utterance have a large part to play in meaning. He even asserts that 'The meaning of a word is entirely determined by its context. In fact there are as many meanings of a word as there are contexts of its usage' (Matejka and Titunik 1986: 79). He goes on to pursue these points by analysing the blend of direct and indirect speech in the novel which creates its characteristic 'Free Indirect Speech' (usually abbreviated to FIS). But he does so in broad terms without moving on to the kind of precise linguistic analysis of recent 'linguistic criticism' which attempts to produce a codification of the mechanics of FIS (e.g. change of tense and person of verbs; and adverbs of time and place) and other significant linguistic features which are usually overlooked by literary critics.

Volosinov/Bakhtin stressed the significance of time and therefore tense when he borrowed the word 'chronotope' from a lecture on biology in 1925 for his chapter 'Forms of Time and Chronotope in the Novel' in *The Dialogic Imagination*. He writes:

> We will give the name *chronotope* (literally 'time space') to the intrinsic interconnectedness of temporal and spatial relationships that are artistically expressed in literature ... The special meaning it has in relativity theory is not important for our purposes; we are borrowing it for literary criticism almost as a metaphor (almost, but not entirely). What counts for us is the fact that it expresses the inseparability of time and space (time as the fourth dimension of space). (Holquist 1981: 84)

He then makes a 'historical' analysis, as he sees it, of specific chronotopes from the adventure-time chronotope of some Greek literature to the biographical chronotope in Tolstoy. They are characterized in such terms as *crisis, redemptive,* and *threshold,* indicative of particular selections of time and space. This subjective codification is not used here but is cited in order to emphasize that the treatment of time and space is crucial to narrative. As he puts it, 'What is the significance of all these chronotopes? What is most obvious is their meaning for *narrative.* They are the organizing centers for the fundamental narrative events of the novel. The chronotope is the place where the knots of narrative are tied and untied.' (Holquist 1981: 250). He does not, however, go on to deal with the specifically linguistic mechanisms expressive of orientation in time and space and it is by examining these that his insight can be developed. Of course such analysis has to be specific to an individual language. In discussing the relationship between language and ideology it is useful to consider how the 'grammar' or mechanisms of language interact with ideologies in particular instances. This should not only illuminate the complexities of an individual text but possibly provide a diagnostic test of general hypotheses as to the positioning of ideology. Such a consideration of language cannot be carried out effectively in isolation from other meaningful aspects of the text. Other factors generally understood to produce meaning such as symbolism or sequencing, repetition or contrast of events need to be included.

In English, time can be articulated in various ways, some of them not features of grammar. The means may be lexical as in '*today/ tomorrow* is my birthday' or 'the clock is striking *midnight*'. Adverbs may be used such as *then/now, always,* or prepositions such as *before, after, at.* The most obvious means is through modification of verbs to indicate tense though, as will be discussed later, the so-called *present, past* and *future* tenses do not always mean what their names imply. Just as important as the handling of time in the linear sequences of events which structure narrative fiction is the handling of space; and the two interlock. As the axiom has it and as a transatlantic crossing brings home, 'One man's space is another man's time'. Originally spatial terms have sometimes been applied eventually to time: so existing terms referring to time often have an etymological root with a spatial meaning. One important form of interlocking is discernible as *deixis*: the location of an utterance in time and space in relation to its speaker. It can be simply illustrated in terms of the contrast between 'I am here now' and 'he was there then'.

Deixis can be summarized as 'the process of anchoring in the spatio-temporal perspective of the speaker' (Traugott and Pratt 1980: 275) or alternatively as 'the location of persons, objects, events, processes and activities being talked about or referred to, in relation to the space–time concept created by the act of utterance and the participation in it, typically of a single speaker and at least one addressee' (Lyons 1978: 2.637). Interwoven with these spatial and temporal perspectives is the equally significant 'opinion or attitude of the speaker towards the proposition that the sentence expresses or the situation that the proposition describes' (Lyons 1978: 2.452). The kind of opinion or attitude referred to is, in logical terms, one ranging from categorical assertion to remote possibility. There are many means of expressing what is called this *epistemic modality*. Lexical choices are possible such as those between verbs like *think, trust, believe, imagine*; or between adverbs like *possibly, perhaps, certainly*. Occasionally the use of different tense forms is possible as in the former distinction between the present time in 'he *may* come' and the past time in 'he *might* come': the first leaves the question of his coming open-ended; the second can give it a less likely status. And syntactic patterns may be used so that narratorial questions, either alone or, as in *Vanity Fair*, (see chapter 2) combined with other features, may contribute to the overall modality: to the stance of the narrator in relation to the certainty of what is recounted.

The unnoticed or hidden linguistic features which will be dealt with here are therefore not merely sentence patterns but include matters such as tense, mood and modality. All of them are powerful elements inhabiting utterances which are themselves hierarchical in structure and in which the scope or domain of elements is important. It is these elements which I call 'invisible writing' since in interpretations of complete lengthy texts they are not usually taken into account. It is this invisible writing that this study tries to reactivate and to link to the more familiar features dealt with by critics. Six Victorian novels have been chosen which seemed to have prominently recurrent linguistic features or modes. These modes are: questions and modality in *Vanity Fair* (1848); tense in *The Mill on the Floss* (1860) and *Daniel Deronda* (1876); deixis in *Bleak House* (1853); negation in *Tess of the d'Urbervilles* (1891) and *Little Dorrit* (1857). Such distinctively marked texts were not hard to find and the features which distinguish three of them are particularly relevant to all narratives in both prose and verse. The aim here is to identify these elements in each text and to show how they contribute to meanings, since they are peculiarly relevant to the novelistic genre because they deal with the central subjects of time, space and point of view.

The key word here is 'contribute' because it is not being suggested that these submerged features of language work in isolation from other signifying systems in the text. They are simply newly noticed factors in its total significance, working for or against other factors such as imagery, narratorial commentary, juxtapositions of characters or events, and sequencing generally. But their importance is crucial: they provide an initial focus which leads unexpectedly into a revealing awareness of nuances of meaning in the novels discussed.

Further, it is not implied that features such as these always work in the same way and to the same effect wherever they are used. The handling of such matters as tense or negation will be shown to be a matter of delicate tactics leading to often surprising results, as in *Bleak House*. The simple preliminary accounts of the scope of these linguistic basics, illustrated from other literary works, is a way of making explicit the knowledge of them which native speakers have already without knowing it. They are like the phonotactic rules or combinative capacities of distinctive English (or other first language) sounds. Native speakers usually focus on their knowledge of these rules only when doing crosswords. They emerge when the puzzler asks her- or himself questions such as 'if *n* is the second letter of this word I'm looking for, what sounds might (or might not) precede it?' Faced with a sufficient number of such questions, the combinatory rules for English sounds would dawn upon such a native speaker. So the preliminary accounts briefly summarize what can or might be expressed through such mechanisms as questions, negatives, past, present and future tenses.

These major structural elements contribute in large part to the transformation of the presumed 'original' sequence of events into a specific text. The orientation in time and space of the narrator and her/his perspective on the possibility or probability of their account constitute the structure of all novels, an invisible architectural frame. Other features of language may be significant in particular novels but not in all. An example of this is the prominent and recurrent use of negation in

Tess and *Little Dorrit*. Lexical means of a less obvious kind may in any case be used. There is a high degree of flexibility as to scope and emphasis involved in uses of the negative, as will be shown in these two texts.

The six chapters are not chronological since it is not being argued that there is a diachronic development in the mechanisms themselves. The aim is to bring them to light and so to enlarge the study of the language of texts beyond semantics seen merely as a matter of lexis and possibly to provide material for discussion of the relationship between language and ideology.

Questions

2

The question of
Vanity Fair

The question arises: can't we be mistaken in thinking that we
understand a question? (Wittgenstein)

THE frequent questions asked by the narrator in *Vanity Fair* (1848)
are potentiated by those raised by the plot as to crucial events,
motives, emotions and inferences to be drawn from them. What actually happens? Does Becky commit adultery with General Tufto, or Lord
Steyne, or nameless others on her travels? Does she kill Joseph Sedley?
How does she persuade Pitt Crawley to buy diamonds for her? Other
matters too are doubtful. Does Amelia wilfully deceive herself about
her dead husband's merits? Are Dobbin's feelings for her merely infatuation? When does he cease to love her, or does he cease? Does Amelia
really know that Dobbin no longer loves her (if he doesn't)? Would
Becky really be a good woman on £5,000 a year? Is Dobbin's *History of
the Punjaub* an example of his ineffectiveness? Is Miss Swartz represented as a figure of fun or a victim? From the earliest reviews these
questions have been expanded into general issues and a search has been
conducted for clear answers seen as choices between binary alternatives. Does the novel endorse domestic ideology, class inequalities, oppressive colonialism, or not? In the end the language of the text has
always resisted yes/no answers.

Undoubtedly the most striking linguistic feature of *Vanity Fair* is
the multiplicity of interrogative structures. The narrator uses them constantly. Superficially viewed, this should not be surprising in a narrative.
Questions are essentially a narrative and dramatic mode of utterance;

they apparently involve a reactive encounter between individuals; they imply a doubt to be resolved. In brief they are inherently dynamic. This view takes all questions at their face value but there is more to consider than surface. Not everything that precedes a question mark has the same communicative status/illocutionary force. 'Won't you sit down?' 'Have you checked your speed, sir?' 'Do you want me to beat you up?' are request, command and threat respectively. On the other hand, a spoken utterance that looks like a statement will only be an assertion with level intonation: 'You like Picasso – so let's go to the exhibition.' With rising intonation it is a question: 'You like Picasso? *If* you do, let's go to the exhibition.'

Similarly the potential of questions is greater than the capacity to solicit an answer. This can be illustrated briefly in T. S. Eliot's 'The Love Song of J. Alfred Prufrock', in which questions are a dominant feature of the language. It is a poem constructed out of questions and structured around one which is 'overwhelming' but unuttered. It is a series of questions about not asking a question. It consists of the reactions of the speaker, Prufrock, to the thought of asking the thing he cannot ask: the difficulties and drawbacks and the possible consequences of doing so. The unspoken question dominates because from the moment he pleads 'Oh, do not ask, "What is it?"' he stimulates the reader's desire to know what it is. A subsequent string of questions expresses hesitancies and fears about how it might be formulated and how to carry off the asking. 'Do I dare?' ' Do I dare?' – 'Do I dare disturb the universe?', – 'how should I presume?', – 'Then how should I begin?' – 'Shall I say …?' – 'Should I … have the strength …?'

Moving beyond the unutterable, the monologue considers the possible aftermath: the regrets, doubts and anguish (imagined in advance) about having asked it. Prufrock obsessively wonders 'And would it have been worth it after all?' – 'Would it have been worthwhile / To have bitten off the matter …?' – 'And would it have been worth it?' – 'would it have been worthwhile?'. Finally for what he dare not ask he substitutes two trivial questions: 'Shall I part my hair behind?' and 'Do I dare to eat a peach?'

This short text shows the complexities latent in an apparently simple linguistic device. It is already complicated in 'Prufrock' by its occurrence in a monologue: no one provides answers. In Eliot's poem there are three relevant aspects to notice which indicate the potential of questions. First there are revealing suppositions built into Prufrock's many questions. 'Do I dare?' supposes that the act of asking the unspoken question would be a risk requiring daring to undertake it. It also implies that the speaker is doubtful of his ability to brace himself to ask it. 'And how should I begin?' with its supplementary 'Shall I say ...?' assumes that there is more than one possible beginning and that they can be ranked as to best practice. Even the final substitute questions involve assumptions: that Prufrock has enough hair to part behind or to deal with in some other way; that a peach is or might be available, that there are options for him of eating it or not, and that eating it would be an act of daring.

The second aspect of questions in 'Prufrock' that can be seen as giving scope for distinctions depends on the options they appear to offer. Even if no interlocutor is involved they technically provide choices. Some indicate that the only choice is between a negative or an affirmative: 'Do I dare?'. The putative listener could of course refuse the choice and withdraw from the encounter by saying 'I don't know', 'Try it and see', or 'Make up your own mind'. He or she cannot meaningfully offer as an answer: 'The Prince Consort', 'Half-past two', or 'With custard please'. 'Do I dare?' then is a yes/no question. Others offer more scope and do not solicit 'yes' or 'no' as answers. 'How should I presume [to ask this question]?' allows for greater variety because 'How' indicates an unknown quantity. The appropriate answer could be one of several or many: 'By pulling yourself together'; 'By asking it in a letter, not face to face'; 'By asking a friend to do it for you'; 'By thinking of something daring you've done previously'; 'By having a stiff drink' etc. This type can be referred to as an x-question, since x is the familiar algebraic symbol for an unknown quantity.

The third relevant potential of an interrogative construction is that it offers a choice between *posing* and *asking* a question. When we *pose* a question we merely give expression to our doubt about the issue involved. A question of the kind, 'Do I dare to eat a peach?' means 'I wonder whether I dare to eat a peach (and there I stop without asking anyone)?' When we *ask* a question of someone we are both posing it and indicating to the person addressed that they are expected to respond. Prufrock's questions can be read in either way. He may be asking a real or imagined listener or himself for a decision, or he may only be able to wonder fruitlessly about the matter. The interpretation of the poem changes with whether the reader thinks he is posing or asking the questions, and the text refuses to indicate which.

Vanity Fair exploits these varying aspects of interrogations and in one instance the introduction of this destabilizing mode is illustrated by a textual change described by Shillingsburg (1993: 11). He points out how an exact account of motivation in the manuscript can be seen to be replaced by a single ironic question. Sir Pitt is commenting on his son Pitt's wish to preach at his aunt; and fears that, if he does so, her money will be bequeathed outside the family. The manuscript reads '"What is money compared to our souls, Sir?" continued Crawley who knew he was not to inherit a shilling of his aunt's money.' There follows a reply from his father and a narratorial comment:

> 'You mean that the old lady won't leave the money to you' – this was in fact the meaning of Mr. Crawley. No man for his own interest could accommodate himself to circumstances more. In London he would let a great man talk and laugh and be as wicked as he liked: but as he could get no good from Miss Crawley's money why compromise his conscience? There was another reason why he should hate Rawdon Crawley. He thought his brother robbed him. Elder brothers often do think so; and curse the conspiracy of the younger children wh. unjustly deprives them of their fortune.

After 'You mean that the old lady won't leave the money to you', a later version substitutes for this lengthy explanation simply an unanswered x-question: 'and who knows but it *was* Mr. Crawley's meaning' (p. 112). The change illustrates a preferred linguistic mode to which the text constantly reverts.

The narrator's questions, like Prufrock's, frequently make suppositions and they are about society's practices, morals and motivations. In this way they tacitly incorporate generalizations assumed to be familiar to readers and accepted by them:

> What causes respectable parents to take up their carpets, set their houses topsy-turvey and spend a fifth of their year's income in ball suppers and iced champagne? (p. 26)

> What good mother is there who would not commiserate a penniless spinster who might have been my lady and shared four thousand a year? (p. 186)

> He was a little wild: how many young men are; and don't girls like a
> rake better than a milksop? (p. 148)

These questions involve general assumptions about the practices of
parents with marriageable daughters, avarice in mothers, and the frequency of 'wildness' in young men. But they also assume that manipulative parents are 'respectable', avaricious mothers are 'good' mothers
and all non-rakes are milksops. The begging of these latter questions
complicates the issue of what is being implied. Is the implication that
this sort of behaviour in parents and mothers is quite compatible with
respectability and maternal virtue and that there is a sense in which
virtuous young men *are* all milksops? These and other questions from
the narrator in *Vanity Fair* are usually of the open-ended x-type (allowing for a range of possible answers). If they are rhetorical questions of
the yes/no type, like the third example, this confuses the issue as to
which is the appropriate answer. As Wittgenstein says of interrogative
forms, 'Can't we be mistaken in thinking that we understand a question?'.

Combined with questions are many other devices that work to
the same effect and dissolve certainty over motives and events. After
Becky's public disgrace with Lord Steyne, the narrator wonders 'the
late fair tenant of that poor little mansion was in the meanwhile –
where?' (p. 705). This asks apparently for a specific place to be named
but goes on to list a series of reported sightings: she has followed
Lord Steyne to Naples; she is living in a Bierstadt and has become
lady-in-waiting to the Queen of Bulgaria; she has gone to Boulogne;
she is living in a Cheltenham boarding house. No choice is made
from these possible locations, so uncertainty is enhanced.

Like 'The Love Song of J. Alfred Prufrock', *Vanity Fair* is a narrative
monologue. There is no stable interlocutor, though there are many
direct addresses to reader(s), male and female: as 'brother wearers of
motley' (p. 227), 'dear M- friend of my youth' (p. 599), 'brother'
(p. 321), 'ladies' (p. 491), 'my kind reader' (p. 95), 'good-natured reader'
(p. 60), 'every reader of a sentimental turn' (p. 179), 'the astonished
reader' (p. 543), and so on. Such readers are never more than transient
figments of the narrator's imagination. Consequently the dynamic force
of the question, referred to initially, its power to initiate a linear progression through an exchange with another person, is removed. Instead

the layers of possible answers blur and diffuse the narrative line and problematize characters.

The novel does not fall neatly into the heterodiegetic or the homodiegetic type of narration in which the questioning narrator is entirely outside the story or entirely within it. He is a spectator present at some few events and also a free floating outsider. His is just one report of the scandalous goings on in the Fair, with little more authority than the rest. Its claim to accuracy is effectively diminished when the narrator locates himself at the dinner-table among other gossips and scandalmongers: 'It was at the little comfortable ducal town of Pumpernickel ... that I first saw Colonel Dobbin and his party ... Everybody remarked the majesty of Jos' (p. 793). Though present at this trivial event, he was clearly not on the scene of the major happenings. This is emphasized by the fact that, at points, he claims to be reduced to guesswork, particularly about Becky: '*I am inclined to think* that there was a period in Mrs. Becky's life when she was seized not by remorse but by a kind of despair and absolutely neglected her person and even her reputation' (p. 813). Such a story-teller identifies himself as one among the others around him who also speculate. He is only rarely an eye-witness and for the rest of the time a channel for reports. The smokescreen of speculation and gossip over who does what and why in *Vanity Fair* casts doubt on the veracity of the narrative itself.

Further, the self-referentiality of the text constantly foregrounds its own fictiveness. The narrator preens himself on handling imagined reader-reaction or on his ability to transpose his story into different genres: 'Jos Sedley is in love with Rebecca. Will he marry her? That is the great subject now in hand'. He might, he says, have treated it 'in the genteel, or in the romantic, or in the facetious manner' (p. 60). Synopses of alternatives follow in which the lover is turned genteelly into 'Lord Joseph Sedley', in the entirely low style into 'black Sambo', and horrifically into 'a professional burglar and murderer who is nameless' (pp. 60–1). In addition, the pervasive irony serves to increase doubt and ambiguity, particularly when narratorial questions are involved. In the passage sometimes read as degrading Becky once and for all when describing her as a mermaid, she is said to be 'singing and smiling, coaxing and cajoling' whilst through the transparent waves her 'hideous and slimy' tail is visible (p. 812). The narrator continues by asking whether or not everything above the waterline everything has not been

'proper, agreeable and decorous; and has any the most squeamish im-
moralist in Vanity Fair a right to cry fie?' (pp. 812–13). As irony always
does, the passage raises the question of what, other than the literal
interpretation, might be meant as to the narrator's perspective, Becky's
behaviour and the implied reader. Such layered irony diffuses meaning
as cataract in the eye diffuses light. It is not just the question that we do
not understand but the apparently implied answer.

The many ironic questions posed by the narrator, the ambiguous
role of the narrator who is internal yet external to the story, the gaps in
knowledge of events and motivation, the substitution of speculation
for fact, and the self-referentiality of the text create a specific epistemic
modality. This indicates the attitude of the teller to the string of statements and judgements that constitute the text. As this account has
shown, the attitude is one of varying degrees of doubt. Even the events
in the Fair which are the evidence for evaluations and judgements are
uncertain in their nature and so in their significance. Hence the modality of the text is 'dubitative'; and the various devices described above,
particularly the question, contribute to it. All reports and judgements
are provisional and subject to doubt. This is the architectural framework of the text.

The propositions or perspectives doubtfully proposed are concerned
with three interlocked areas: gender, social class and race/nationalism.
The three issues all involve a power hierarchy, the dominance over others which is a determinant and validation of identity: men over women,
upper- and middle-classes over the working class, and the English/Brit-
ish over other nations, French or Oriental. The discourses that author-
ize these systems of power do so by representing the last two as parallel
to the first. As Cixous puts it, 'Subordination of the feminine to the
masculine order … gives the appearance of being the condition of the
machinery's functioning' (Wing 1986: 65). The gender hierarchy was
in this discourse presented as part of the natural order: evolution had
enhanced female procreative capacity at the expense of the development
of rational powers. By analogy factory workers, labourers and servants
could be represented as in need, like women, of what Carlyle in *Chartism*
(1839) called 'governance' by superior beings: 'One select class Society
has furnished with wealth, intelligence, leisure, means outward and
inward for governing; another huge class, furnished by Society with
none of these things, declares that it must be governed' (Shelston 1986:

197). By the same analogy other nations were represented as infantile and/or deviant depending on whether they were African, Oriental or European. Governing or resisting them was a duty not an oppression.

Like all ideological constructs, this one was in flux. There were direct challenges from individuals like Harriet Martineau, though they did not all take the same form. She questioned in particular the insistence on the solely domestic nature of women's role and the limits it placed on their education: 'women who are furnished with but one object – marriage – must be as unfit for anything when their aim is accomplished as if they had never had any object at all'. Where they are educated with other aims in view 'their independence of mind places them beyond the reach of the spoiler' (Yates, 1985: 61). Nor was the ideology unchanging. As Judith Newton points out while distinguishing a shift which took place in the 1840s: 'Much feminist criticism, although it assumes the existence of unequal gender-based relations of power, implicitly constructs those relations in such a way as to render them tragic – unchanging, universal and monolithically imposed (Bostock 1987: 125). By contrast she shows how in the decade from 1840 to 1850, 'the hungry forties', as social unrest exemplified by the Chartist movement grew, women were able to adapt their sphere in a way that authorized an extension of their influence. Their role as moral guardians was a mainstay of the construction of femininity. A man needs, as Ellis's *Wives of England* puts it:

> a companion who will be supremely solicitous for the advancement
> of his intellectual, moral, and spiritual nature; a companion who will
> raise the tone of his mind from low anxieties, and vulgar cares which
> necessarily occupy so large a portion of his existence, and lead his
> thoughts to expatiate or repose on the subjects which convey a feel-
> ing of identity with a higher state of existence beyond this present
> life. (Ellis 1843a: 100)

By a natural extension this moral mission could encompass compassion for the deprived. The poor were normally regarded as unable to speak articulately for themselves. Carlyle in 1839 speaks of 'Dingy dumb millions, grimed with dust and sweat, with darkness, rage and sorrow' who struggle to cry out the words he utters for them 'Behold our lot is unfair; our life is not whole but sick; we cannot live under injustice' (Shelston, 1986: 217). Women could naturally offer themselves, as

Gaskell does in the Preface to *Mary Barton* (1848), as mouthpieces 'to give some utterance to the agony which, from time to time, convulses this dumb people' such as those whom Gaskell passes in the streets of Manchester. Domestic fiction of the period provides models of women in this missionary role on behalf of the working class. Caroline Helstone in Charlotte Brontë's *Shirley* (1848) and Margaret Hale in Elizabeth Gaskell's *North and South* (1854) are middle-class women who reform recalcitrant capitalistic lovers by winning them over to paternalistic compassion for their 'hands'. Both women effect appropriately domestic improvement: new housing for workers, and a communal factory kitchen. The amelioration of working-class conditions, to which the danger of civil disorder drove the establishment, could thus be appropriated by women. By the 1860s this extension of feminine influence was challenged.

In the 1840s, however, this ideological shift seemed to allow women to see themselves as having a hand in changes such as those brought about in housing by the Municipal Corporations Act of 1835 and the beginning of improvements in sanitation through the Public Health Act of 1848. As will appear in chapter 3, one challenge to such feminine territorial expansion took the form of a counter-ideal of masculinity not influenced by the weaker 'feminine' virtues but, as Newton says, less 'effeminate', more autonomous, self-sufficient, unemotional, physically robust 'manliness' (Bostock 1987: 134).

The use of the feminine–masculine hierarchy to trope class, national and racial power-relations accounts for the centrality of the Amelia–Becky pairing in *Vanity Fair*. Alternative perspectives are continuously on offer. Comparison apparently in Amelia's favour is initiated by the quest in the opening chapters for a heroine in this 'novel without a hero'. In chapter two she is described as 'the heroine of this work' on account of her amiability and her 'humble and gentle temper' (p. 15). Her standing as feminine prototype is recognized by her iconic status as honorary colonel-in-chief when she joins 'her regiment' at Chatham after marrying George Osborne, 'invades the Low Countries' and embarks on the road to George's death at Waterloo. She is recognized as the perfect wife by the 'honest young fellows of the -th regiment' for whom it becomes the fashion to 'adore and admire' Mrs. Osborne on account of her 'artless behaviour ... simplicity and sweetness' (pp. 325–6). These characteristics are confirmed by her selfless concern for her bankrupt and difficult parents, her fidelity to her dead husband despite his dalliance with Becky on their honeymoon, and her sacrifice of her son to his wealthy and hostile paternal grandfather.

The narrator, however, in practice alternates between what appears to be genuine approval and equally genuine contempt for a woman 'made by nature for a victim' who characteristically has 'recourse to the waterworks'. At moments both perspectives are on offer simultaneously. There is the option of reading as ingenuous or ironic the x-question posed by the narrator at the point where Amelia becomes the wonder of the -th regiment: 'But who has not beheld these among women and *recognized* the presence of all sorts of qualities in them, even though they say no more to you than that they are engaged to dance the next quadrille, or that it is very hot weather?' (p. 326). Is this a tribute to the men who recognize Amelia's merits and acknowledge them or is it a joke at the expense of men's inability to see the vacuity that appearances rightly point to?

Amelia in most circumstances is a burden not an asset, 'heart' without 'head', as reviewers often pointed out. This is particularly clear in her journey to Brussels and its aftermath. She represents not the modified version of 1840s' 'femininity' that Newton describes but the unreconstructed form without an extra-domestic influence. Thackeray, resisting this new influence when describing a woman's intervention in a discussion of the state of Ireland, writes to a woman friend in 1848 'I'm afraid I dont respect your sex enough though. – Yes I do when they are occupied with loving and sentiment rather than with other business of life' (Ray 1945–46: 2.438). But this pro-Amelia view is contradicted by a letter to his mother four months earlier when he refers casually to the fact that 'Arthur and his pretty, nice amiable milksop Amelia sort of wife go to India next month' (Ray 1945–46: 2.383). Similarly in *Vanity Fair* the narrator's dual account of Amelia poses in effect a restricted x-question: 'Is Amelia an ideal woman – or is she contemptible?'

Becky is the other side of femininity, the dangerous one, and increasingly attractive to all, including the narrator. She is not English but half-French; not middle-class but obliged to earn a living as an unclassed governess; not selfless but motivated shamelessly by self-interest shrewdly and vigorously pursued. It follows naturally from this triply undesirable identity that her ambiguous relationships with General

Tufton, George Osborne, Lord Steyne and Joseph Sedley mark her as a sexual deviant. She even combines the status of fallen woman with that of the equally disreputable actress. As a male character in an exactly contemporary novel says 'A woman who makes her mind public ... or exhibits herself in any way ... seems to me little better than a woman of a nameless class' (Jewsbury 1848: 2.18–19). Becky is just such a woman who has inherited histrionic talents from her mother, the French 'opera-dancer'. She displays them in brilliant performances of charades at Gaunt House in the parts of Clytemnestra and 'the most *ravissante* little marquise' (p. 650). Both are foreigners, respectively a murderer and a coquette of dubious morality. When bored by 'good society' she hankers shamelessly for the spotlight and forbidden excitement of public performance: 'oh, how much gayer it would be to wear spangles and dance before a booth at a fair' (p. 638). Later she makes a living abroad out of publicizing projected performances that she never gives. All things French from Napoleon to their actresses were commonplace signs for the degraded and corrupt. 'Vive la France! Vive l'empereur!' (p. 14) cries Becky, after her first triumph over the Misses Pinkerton, in ironic celebration of her allegiances. Or as a contemporary reviewer put it 'the construction of this little clever monster is diabolically French' (Tillotson and Hawes 1968: 85).

Her diabolical Frenchness has serious features, however. The charades at Gaunt House subsequently appear proleptic in their foreshadowing of illicit sex and murder. Rawdon Crawley returns unexpectedly from the debtors' prison to find her 'in brilliant full toilette ... the brilliants on her breast which Steyne had given her' (p. 675). He reads the signs as readily as any Victorian reader would: they indicate adultery. He does not even have to express his thought for Becky to cry, 'I am innocent'. Similarly there are indications that she acts the role of a murderous Clytemnestra to Jos Sedley's Agamemnon. There is Thackeray's own illustration of Dobbin's last visit to Sedley, showing Becky lurking grimly behind a curtain, entitled 'Becky's Second Appearance in the Character of Clytemnestra' (opposite p. 874). After Jos's death, the life insurance company refuses payment.

But these most damning of Becky's 'acts' are only supposed as possibilities, or rather 'posed' as questions as to the fact, to which no answer is required or given. After Rawdon's discovery of her with Steyne the narrator 'poses' a string of such questions: 'What *had* happened? Was she guilty or not? She said not; but who could tell what was the truth which came from those lips; or if that corrupt heart was in this case pure?' (p. 677). It now appears uncertain, even to him, what has happened. The proposition that Becky had committed adultery is offered only doubtfully, as the passage oscillates between a guilty and a not-guilty verdict. The same retrospective destabilizing occurs with the death of Jos Sedley. His life insurance company claims that the circumstances are deeply suspicious – but they would say that wouldn't they? Becky's lawyers, however, are successful, 'The money was paid and her character established' (p. 877). This is a characteristically ambiguous comment: is it asserting Becky's innocence or merely making an ironically legalistic point? One contemporary reviewer could certainly read it as exonerating her and compares her favourably with two known poisoners:

> The genus of Pigeon and Laffarge claims her for its own – only that our heroine takes a far higher class by not requiring the vulgar matter of fact of crime to develop her full powers. It is an affront to Becky's tactics to believe that she could ever be reduced to so low a resource ... We, therefore, cannot sufficiently applaud the extreme discretion with which Mr. Thackeray has hinted at the possibly assistant circumstances of Joseph Sedley's dissolution. (Tillotson and Hawes 1968: 85)

Another reader, Dickens's editor, John Forster, could take an opposite view and wrote disapprovingly that 'She commits every conceivable wickedness: dishonours her husband, betrays her friend, degrades and embrutes herself, and finally commits a murder' (Tillotson and Hawes 1968: 56).

To complicate the issue further, Becky, in spite of her negative ideological overload, as Norton (1993: 133) points out, shadows the contemporary ideal of femininity. She uses her intuitive powers to assess the needs and desires of those she deals with and then her histrionic talent to satisfy them. Her 'feminine' adaptability is impressive. With the revolting old Sir Pitt Crawley she can be housekeeper, entertainer, pacifier, support, land agent: keeping him happy and advising on the felling of timber, the harvesting of crops and all without shaking his *amour propre*. With the rich and snobbish Miss Crawley she can intuit how to be the perfect companion, satisfying her patron's greed for rich food and malicious gossip, without disturbing the woman's necessary sense of social superiority. In addition to making (rich) old people happy she can transform Rawdon Crawley's life when (to reverse the usual subject and object) *she* marries *him*. He is for some time happy in the possession of a perfect wife who provides what Ellis calls a necessary 'choice of every personal indulgence' (1843a: 91–2). 'I'm no angel', she says, flaunting her unwomanly status, but knowing she is well able to display the domestic angel's skills. In addition to satisfying Rawdon's domestic and sexual needs, Becky effects the kind of moral improvement a virtuous English wife was supposed to produce. The 'heavy dragoon' gives up most of his vices such as gambling (except under her supervision to earn a livelihood) as well as his now unnecessary mistresses, the 'milliners' and 'opera dancers' (p. 365). By achieving this Becky out-Amelias Amelia so as to upset the balance sheet between the two.

In this way the overall epistemic modality problematizes Becky's value along with Amelia's. She is Amelia's defining Other in that she is lower-class, though sexually deviant and selfish. But she is an anomaly in that she outdoes Amelia in feminine plasticity and domestic skills. And she deviates strikingly from the prototype of fallen woman by lacking utterly the shame appropriate to her condition, which erodes most fictional fallen women of the period. Despite a momentary and histrionic impulse to solve her problems with a dose of laudanum, she never follows the fictional convention which requires a woman like her to regard suicide by drowning as a suitable self-punishment and cleansing. She is one of the very few characters in the novel without a shred of the self-deceit of which *Vanity Fair* exhibits such an extensive repertoire. Because of these contradictions in her representation, she ceases to be the kind of generic character figured by the naturalness of converting Amelia's name to a common noun, 'an amelia'. Becky will always be upper case, never 'a magdalen'. In one aspect she shows the danger of the then recent assertions as to the propriety of extending female influence outside the family. She is a 'loose' canon in both senses of the word. In another aspect she is an example of the contestation by a few of the contemporary construction of 'femininity'. This challenge is made by Harriet Martineau when in 1851 she expressed views similar to those of John Stuart Mill, stressing the need for a recognition that woman is not unitary. She predicted a time when it would be plainly absurd to everyone to argue as was then being done 'about what woman ought to do, before it was ascertained what woman can do' (Yates, 1985: 75). Becky achieves the individuality which is a precondition of equality. The problematic nature of Becky's identity is recognized by at least one contemporary reviewer who compares her with Jane Eyre:

> They do not fit into any ready-made criticism. They give the most stupid something to think of, and the most reserved something to say; the most charitable too are betrayed into home comparisons which they usually condemn, and the most ingenious stumble into paradoxes which they can hardly defend. (Tillotson and Hawes 1968: 78)

The same reviewer also admires Becky as someone who, though she is the devil's offspring, can invariably distinguish 'those decencies which more virtuous, but more stupid humanity, often disclaims'. For example she reveres Dobbin 'in spite of his big feet' (p. 83). The text holds these contradictory versions of Becky in tension by offering each as plausible but uncertain. The epistemic mode is throughout realized as dubitative, unsettled and unsettling. She is wickedly unscrupulous and therefore to be condemned but wonderfully successful as entrepreneur and charmer and therefore to be admired.

Becky's problematic status has consequences for the practice of using the masculine–feminine hierarchy as a naturalizing model for the power relations of social classes. This difficulty was exacerbated by the fact that acute fear of social unrest in the 1840s generated by the industrial discontent which culminated in the Chartist movement was combined with a recognition of genuine reasons for such discontent. As the condition-of-England novels show, a middle-class awareness of privation and glaring inequalities had developed along with government Blue Books on sanitation, housing and mortality rates. In addition, so too had a sense of guilt. Carlyle in his essay on 'Chartism' (1839) recognizes that the condition of the working classes is indeed a question: 'Is the condition of the English working people wrong; so wrong that rational working men cannot, will not, and even should not rest quiet?' (Shelston, 1986: 152). Thackeray too sees the injustice of contemporary society as a 'problem'. He writes in a letter of 1848: 'I am certain that wealth is good for the poor: and feel sure that any change in the division of it, would only end in some such similar and seemingly partial scheme as that which at present revolts us' (Ray 1945–46: 2.236). This statement is already contradictory: the current organization of wealth is revolting and yet only '*seemingly* partial' (my emphasis). He has an evident fear of social upheaval which he expresses as a question in a later letter: 'The great revolution is a coming a coming ... our young ones may live to see awful changes but what?' (Ray 1945–46: 2.762–3). This fear is compounded by moral insecurity: many recognized their society as essentially unjust but could not bear to contemplate change – no alternative seemed personally bearable and no salve for a sense of guilt was readily available in the shape of a morality explaining what was supposed to hold society together. Both at home and in the colonies British society displayed the lack of any set of descriptive terms which purported to describe it as a coherent whole. It was, as the historian Geoffrey Crossick says, 'anomic' (Corfield 1991: 160).

For many of the middle and upper classes during the unrest of the 1840s, servants, not farm labourers or factory workers, were the threat to social stability closest at hand and a (largely invisible) example of the growing inequality of society. Ellis spells out the extreme view of them. The best 'are too much under the influence of false and limited views of things in general, to admit of their being desirable companions for children in their moments of unrestrained confidence'. The worst are 'artful and unprincipled characters' (Ellis 1843b: 247). By corrupting their masters' children, servants can act as a Trojan rocking-horse in the domestic circle. The scene among the servants in Curzon Street after the break up of Becky's marriage figures this threat. So too does the earlier scene when Isidor, Jos Sedley's Belgian servant longs for the moment when Napoleon's triumph will make his master's expensive accoutrements legally his – as he holds a (shaving) razor to Jos's throat. Both episodes show the working classes as a danger equatable with that which Becky represents; and yet both are invested with a bacchanalian glee which the narrator shares. The servants, like Becky the ex-governess, take the more equal distribution of wealth into their own hands. At the same time there is a certain pleasure to be gained from the sight of Becky's servants helping themselves to her maraschino and dipping their fingers into her cream dish when Rawdon leaves her.

But the fear that envy and violence towards their superiors was latently endemic in all servants, even Sir Pitt Crawley's apparently faithful nurse who bullies him in private, is countered by the representation of Becky's landlord Raggles and her 'sheepdog' companion Miss Briggs.

Both are cheated of their savings and livelihood by Becky and Rawdon as a result of trusting to their honesty. Their pathetic misery enacts an alternative view that injustice is inherent in a society where it is a gentleman's prerogative 'to live on nothing a year'. This translated means at the expense of tradesmen and servants. Thackeray refers to such injustice when advising an acquaintance who is heavily in debt to leave the country: 'Going to prison will not discharge your great or small debts. One of the bitterest of all bitter mortifications you will have to endure, will be this leaving the servants and poor tradesmen with their claims unsatisfied' (Ray 1945–46: 2.236). As with Becky's character, opposing positions on the working classes are offered. They are like unruly children who rampage while their parents (employers) are away. On the other hand, they are loyal and trusting retainers preserving moral values in a society largely without such values. Looked at from another viewpoint, Raggles and Miss Briggs are ludicrous as well as pathetic in a gullibility that springs from a kind of stupidity.

The representation of imperialism also involves a parallel with the domestic economy: an assumption of racial and national superiority like that of men over women. The casual nature of this belief in the text is telling. There is an implication that the matter does not need to be spelt out; the coded view is already in place to be alluded to. The Sedleys call their black servant 'Sambo', a name given pejoratively from the eighteenth century onwards to those assumed to be of African descent. It erases the individual's identity and creates a generic name that can be given to all black replacements. George Osborne refers to the West Indian heiress Rhoda Swartz and Amelia's schoolfellow as as 'that mulatto woman' and a 'Hottentot Venus' (p. 259), the stage name of a black woman who appeared on display in London during the period 1810–15. She was notable for the huge size of her buttocks (Thomas 1992: 1–5). But since the Sedleys and Osbornes are themselves savagely criticized, their racism can scarcely be seen as underwritten by Thackeray. Some clue as to his view of black races is found in a letter of 1848 where he tells how his 'black niece … daughter of a natural sister of mine' wrote to his mother when she visited Europe for the first time as 'her "dear Grandmama"' and adds 'Fancy the astonishment of that dear majestic old woman!' (Ray 1945–46: 2.367). The narrator himself in *Vanity Fair* makes similarly casual assumptions of racial superiority: Rhoda Swartz is repeatedly referred to as 'woolly-haired', a derogatory term for the curly hair of Africans. It alternated with 'woolly-headed' which had a secondary meaning of 'stupid'; and it may also have carried this suggestion of stupidity. The conventional view that blacks were fascinated by trinkets, bright colours and finery is alluded to in the description of her dress as she waits for George: 'her favourite amber-coloured satin, with turquoise-bracelets, countless rings, flowers, feathers, and all sorts of tags and gimcrack, about as elegantly decorated as a chimney sweep on Mayday' (p. 252). Thackeray's illustration shows her huge and thick-lipped at the piano. This reveals, according to physiognomists, that she has, like all black people, 'a facile nature' (Walker 1834: 257). She responds to Amelia's departure from school with 'downright hysterics' and 'a passion of tears' (p. 7), and to the Osbornes' flattery with 'quite a tropical ardour'.

The brutal racism of parts of the text is countered, as is the view on class, however, by the perspective on the representatives of racial superiority, who make a ludicrous showing: Jos Sedley, Mrs O'Dowd, Fake, Fogle and Cracksman are unlikely exemplars of a superior race. This leaves only Dobbin, part of the occupying force and a man who spends his retirement writing a never completed *History of the Punjaub*. By the mid-nineteenth century the yardstick in discussions of moral superiority was 'gentlemanliness'. Thackeray's narrator claims to use this concept as a way of identifying moral (and social) superiority when he raises the question: 'Which of us can point out many such in his circle – men whose aims are generous, whose truth is constant ... whose want of meanness makes them simple: who can look the world honestly in the face with an equal manly sympathy for the great and for the small ... of gentlemen how many?' (p. 792). The narrator's only nominee is Dobbin and the implication of this rhetorical x-question seems to be that such men are rare. But the terms in which the accolade is awarded to Dobbin are doubtful: 'his thoughts were just, his brains were fairly good, his life was honest and pure, and his heart warm and humble. He certainly had very large hands and feet ...' (p. 792). Is this minimalism a match with the standard laid down? Are fairly good brains enough? And why stress the grotesque hands and feet just now? Not to mention the 'very long legs, yellow face and a slight lisp, which was at first ridiculous' referred to immediately before the standard is defined? Further complicating the issue is the restricted question requiring the answer 'yes' which follows the statement that Osborne's sneers at Dobbin's ludicrous appearance misled Amelia: 'But have we not all been misled about our heroes and changed our opinions a hundred times?' Dobbin's status is later again destabilized, suggesting such a possible revision of opinion. His moment of real honesty when he rightly rejects the maudlin Amelia as not worthy of his love is compromised by his immediate return to her when she summons him. Knowledge of the world and an absence of weakness are an absolute requirement for respect from the narrator in this text. His final address to the united pair as the 'tender little parasite' and 'honest William' reveals, by its use of the minimalist meaning of 'honest' (OED *honest* 1a), a distaste for the first and a degree of patronizing approval for the second such as infuriates its recipient Iago when Othello calls him 'honest, honest Iago'.

The supposed superiority of the colonizers becomes a joke. It is emphasized by Mrs Major O'Dowd who processes through India as Queen Empress (a title not given to Victoria by Disraeli until 1876). She rides at the head of the regiment 'on a royal elephant, a noble sight … she has been received by the native princes who have welcomed her and Glorvina into the recesses of their zenanas [i.e. harems] and offered her shawls and jewels which it went to her heart to refuse' (p. 543). In practice the 'superior' race occupies itself with trivia: manoeuvres, matchmaking, tea-drinking, balls and gossip and liaisons. It is army life in its usual form encamped on an invisible sub-continent. The real India is glimpsed only subliminally in the discomfort and loneliness it imposes on Jos as Collector (of revenues) at Boggley Wollah 'a fine, lonely, marshy, jungly district' (p. 27).

Empire is a fantasy world which is geographically transferable. When they have built up their fortunes in India, Jos and his associates relocate India in a very specific area of London 'of which Moira Place is the centre' surrounded by Great Clive Street, Warren Street and Hastings Street. 'Who' asks the narrator in an ironic x-question 'does not know these abodes of the retired Indian aristocracy?' (p. 761). The new 'India' is a replica of the London merchant hierarchy veiled in oriental glamour and baptized with colonizers' names, but built upon the same basis of financial chicanery. Jos buys his furniture there from the estate of the bankrupt Mr Scape [?Scapegoat]:

> lately admitted partner into the great Calcutta house of Fogle [i.e. pickpocket], Fake, and Cracksman [i.e. housebreaker], in which poor

> Scape had embarked seventy thousand pounds, the earnings of a
> long and honourable life, taking Fake's place, who returned to a
> princely park in Sussex ... admitted, I say, partner to the great agency
> house of Fogle and Fake two years before it failed for a million, and
> plunged half the Indian public into misery and ruin. (pp. 761–2)

In the course of the century the Empire had signified many different things. It was seen as the object of a civilizing or christianizing
mission, an arena for military glory, a manifestation of racial superiority, a focus of national identity and pride. It was also, as in *Vanity Fair*,
a recognized source of materials and commodities. In this text it enacts
what Earl Grey described in 1853 as 'the old doctrine that the great
value of the colonies arises from the commercial monopoly which the
mother country can claim with respect to their trade'. From this
Aladdin's cave of desirable objects both civil and military colonizers like
Jos and Dobbin bring gifts of cashmere shawls, ivory chessmen (p. 495),
pickles and preserves (p. 496). Becky fantasizes about the Orient as a
source of luxurious commodities as she dresses for dinner with Jos Sedley:
'she had built for herself a most magnificent castle in the air ... she had
arrayed herself in an infinity of shawls, turbans and diamond neck-
laces, and had mounted upon an elephant to the sound of the march in
Bluebeard in order to pay a visit of ceremony to the Grand Mogul' (pp.
26–7). The fictive, constructed nature of Empire as slave and luxury,
jungle and treasure house, is highlighted in the melodramatic charade
at Gaunt House when a slave merchant presents a veiled female: 'A
thrill of applause bursts through the house. It is Mrs. Winkworth (she
was a Miss Absolom) with the beautiful hair and eyes. She is in a gorgeous
oriental costume; the black braided locks are twined with innumerable
jewels; her dress is covered with gold piastres' (pp. 664–5).

Historians explain the anomic society of home and empire as a result of the disappearance of an earlier representation of social groupings: society as a hierarchy of ranks. This system had been held in place
by moralistic assumptions about the rights and duties of individuals
and the efficacy of such a system. Benevolence was supposed to trickle
down from rank to rank, and service to pass equally efficiently upward,
providing identity, role and appropriate expectations for all. Such a
representation could not be adapted to provide an ideological naturali-
zation of an industrial society as it had done for a primarily agricultural

one. By the end of the first decade of the nineteenth century the acceptance of society as 'ranked' had given way to the perception of three groups/classes, though the term *rank* could still be used as an alternative to *class* without reference to the earlier framework. The classes were seen to be based on socio-economic functions: labour, capital and property. These terms, transferred from activities and objects to people, indicate the criteria for the new social classification. People were what they did or what they owned: all were parts of a single machine for producing and circulating commodities. This mechanistic account of society, derived from the writings of political economists like David Ricardo (whose *Principles of Political Economy* was published in 1817), was the over-riding metaphor for society's framework. Since their connection was represented as purely economic, the assumption was, as Ruskin wrote later in *Unto this Last* (1903: 114), 'Moral considerations [have] nothing to do with political economy. Therefore moral considerations have nothing to do with human capacities and dispositions.'

Both at home and abroad, in capital city and colony, insofar as the text articulates an alternative to society as parts of an economic machine, it is that of a communal and individual libidinal economy. The desire for and pursuit of the products of the economic machine, whether they are commodities, or commodified persons. This provides both a dynamic for the narrative and a constant to which everyone from Isidor to Dobbin relates. Vanity Fair is like its original in Bunyan: a bazaar or marketplace. Becky's initial aspiration to secure a place for herself in a wealthy merchant's family at the cost of selling her person to Jos Sedley focuses this motivating desire to procure and possess. She repeats the attempt unflaggingly throughout the narrative as one wished-for object after another, perhaps temporarily secured, moves out of reach. Many conversely try to buy a share in Becky for diamonds or cash. Osborne senior tries to buy Miss Swartz, the West Indian heiress, first for his son and then for himself, before she is finally sold off for a Scottish title. Even Amelia sells her son, the third George Osborne, to his paternal grandfather in return for money to support her parents; the language of love is money or commodities. As Dickens says in *Hard Times* (1854), love takes 'on all occasions … a manufacturing aspect' (Ford and Monod 1966: 1, chapter 15). Dobbin expresss his love for Amelia with the anonymous gift of her piano bought at her father's bankruptcy sale; Rawdon's concern for Becky on the night before the battle of Waterloo takes the form of leaving her both his horses, dressing-case with gold-topped bottles, pins, rings, watch and chain, driving cloak lined with sable fur, saddle-holsters, duelling pistols and newest uniform (p. 367); Amelia fetishizes first the piano which she thinks has come from George Osborne and later after his death a portrait of him; Dobbin woos the widow with gifts, 'a box of scarfs, and a grand ivory set of chessmen from China … preserves and pickles … a pair of shawls' (pp. 495–6).

But though the text is explicitly critical of those who engage in this ceaseless pursuit of commodities or commodified persons, the natural entrepreneurs like Becky or the financially successful like old Sir Pitt Crawley or George Osborne senior are the most dynamic figures in the narrative. The narrator in practice expresses the same moth-like fascination as everyone else with the successful in the game. Becky is admired for being able to package and sell herself rather be bought. She is also admirably able through her control of Rawdon's gambling skills, as Miller says, to make good use of 'those moments when the dominant system of commodity exchange lapses, when the strict principle of reciprocity at the center of that exchange does not function, and when something may be had for nothing' (Miller 1995: 39). The narrator is subject to the same lusts as the members of society amongst whom from time to time he places himself. This is evident in the procession of glittering delights lovingly described. It is given an uneasy force by turning these into the object of his own personal *ubi sunt*. There is no apparent irony in such laments. As Miller and other critics have recognized, death is repeatedly represented as the ultimate frustration and desolation when the apparent or temporary owner of property drops for ever out of the endless circulation of desired commodities. The bankruptcy sale of a needy merchant is proleptic of his ultimate loss of all his worldly goods when he dies; bodily dissolution is figured by the decay of property: 'How changed the house is though! The front is patched over with bills, setting forth particulars of the furniture in staring capitals. They have hung a shred of carpet out of an upstairs window – a half-dozen of porters are lounging on the dirty steps.' The broad table 'once sparkling with plate and linen' is now presided over by the 'roaring auctioneer' (p. 201). The narrator is moved by the thought of the dying Sedley considering his life in terms of a financial (not moral) balance sheet:

> Perhaps as he was lying awake then, his life may have passed before him – his early hopeful struggles, his manly successes and prosperity, his downfall in his declining years and his present helpless condition – no chance of revenge against Fortune, which had had the better of him – neither name nor money to bequeath – a spent-out, bootless life of defeat and disappointment, and the end here! Which I wonder brother reader, is the better lot, to die prosperous and famous, or poor and disappointed? To have and be forced to yield; or to sink out of life, having played and lost the game? (p. 771)

This is the narrator's (if not Prufrock's) overwhelming question: a restricted x-question offering only two options as to how to view one's lot in life: which is worse, to die prosperous or to die poor and *therefore* as a failure. It expresses an agony over the loss of material prosperity that would have been incompatible with Bunyan's original view of Vanity Fair as a place of worthless bartering. In this it is like many paradoxical *ubi sunts*. Presumably since it locally not only fetishizes but anguishes over the loss of commodities in a romantic fashion, it retrospectively turns the criticism of a commodified society into something uncertainly offered. It articulates the paradox underlying the dubitative mode. It can be seen as a major example of what Miller means when he observes that Thackeray 'remains deeply invested in the processes that produce the multifarious material objects surrounding him. His desire for these goods fully implicates him in the economic system he simultaneously decries' (Miller 1990: 1042). It is perhaps for this reason that Thackeray is unable 'to find the end of the question between property and labour' (Ray 1945–46: 2.356). As a contemporary critic said, 'Always occupied with moral symptoms … he never attempts to decide a moral question' (Tillotson and Hawes 1968: 278). The Bakhtinian account of competing discourses in novelistic language is fully exemplified in *Vanity Fair*. What is also clear is the historically specific nature of the competing voices in a text published between the hungry forties and the Great Exhibition. All relate to a model of society as an economic machine which is represented simultaneously as impoverished in human terms and irresistibly attractive.

Tense

3

Past and present in
The Mill on the Floss

For the Present holds in it both the whole Past and the whole Future (Carlyle, *Past and Present*)

C ARLYLE'S description of the present is characteristically cryptic but it is significant in that it implies its power. It captures the need to consider the significance of the present not only actually but in verbal forms. For tenses in English are not simply linked to the calendar in the way their names suggest. For instance it is usual to assume that the use of a present as opposed to a past tense form, because of its connection with 'now' in the real world, gives immediacy to statements. It can certainly do this in a commentary on an event while it is happening: 'He hits it for six'. Or it can be used to make a past event vivid in colloquial speech: 'then he hits me with this bottle'. But liveliness is not its main function in writing. That function is the authority it can claim for statements which are being made: an assertion that what is said is true at all times or even 'timelessly' true and therefore requires the present tense. Complete certainty is claimed for the statements 'Man is mortal', 'A rolling stone gathers no moss', 'Guinness is good for you' and for multiplication tables. What happens in *The Mill on the Floss* is that the Tullivers' childhood and that of their community is given a dominant significance by the opening chapter which uses the present tense to give it special authority.

As will be shown in chapter 5, in *Bleak House* Dickens deploys the two tenses in a way that contrasts the narrow perspective of Esther with the all-seeing third person narrator. This does not lead to the conclusion that this is the only telling way to use the two tenses. There are others, one of which is discernible in *The Mill on the Floss* (1860). In George Eliot's novel the past and present tense also criss-cross the narration but in different ways and with different results. Dickens in *Barnaby Rudge* (1841) and *A Tale of Two Cities* (1859) is interested in the historical past and its events. Eliot by contrast is centrally concerned with the much broader issue of the relationship of the past to the present, as were many Victorian intellectuals such as Carlyle. They look obsessively towards not just historic time but prehistoric time. In handling the subject in this novel, Eliot does not use the two tenses as Dickens does but in a more complex way which reverses expectations.

It is necessary first to outline the Victorian treatment of past and present time in various disciplines in order to recognize the debate with which Eliot is engaging. The attitudes of imaginative writers and scientists constitute two contrasting strands in the contemporary treatment of how the past relates to the present. Firstly the upheavals of industrialization were accompanied by a romantic nostalgia for the past, evident in poetry and painting. This often took the form of a yearning for an earlier society that was supposed to be idyllically integrated and morally pristine. Such a society was sometimes figured in Wordsworthian terms as an individual's paradisal childhood. As well as being found in poetry, such Edenic colouring of early life is present even in autobiographies of the time. Charles Darwin (1809–82) wrote in 1838 of a holiday by the sea when he was ten years old: 'The memory now flashes across me of the pleasure I had in the evening on a blowy day walking along the beach by myself and seeing the gulls and cormorants wending their way home in a wild and irregular course. Such poetic pleasures felt so keenly in after years, I should not have expected so early in life' (de Beer 1974: 6–7).

John Ruskin (1819–1900) describes a similarly rapturous recollection in *Praeterita: Outlines of Scenes and Thoughts perhaps Worthy of Memory in my Past life*. Writing of the garden of his father's house in Herne Hill, he says: 'The differences of primal importance which I observed between the nature of this garden, and that of Eden, as I had imagined it, were, that, in this one, *all* the fruit was forbidden; and there were no companionable beasts: in other respects the little domain answered every purpose of Paradise to me' (Cockshut 1994: 23). The two figures of a past society or childhood as Eden fell easily together because of the connection made between ontogeny and phylogeny: between the pattern of development of an individual and that of a society, which it was supposed to mirror.

Predictably the past society which individual writers chose as their Golden Age reflected their personal preferences. To John Ruskin it appeared that 'Great nations write their autobiographies in three manuscripts – the book of their deeds, the book of their words, and the book of their art.' Of the three he believes 'the only quite trustworthy one is the last' (Clark 1964: 196). Consequently for him the ideal society in the past is that enshrined in the paintings, sculptures and buildings created in the Renaissance period in continental Europe. Matthew Arnold's choice is the age of the 'best art and poetry of the Greeks, in which religion and poetry are one, in which the idea of beauty and of a human nature perfect on all sides adds to itself a religious and devout energy' (Lipman 1994: 37). Later, for William Morris the ideal past society was that of the Middle Ages when workmen produced objects of use and beauty with their own hands, something impossible in his own industrialized 'profit-grinding society' (Le Quesne, Landow, Collini and Stansky 1993: 363). All three, Ruskin, Arnold and Morris, not only idealize an earlier society but share a belief that such a society is inscribed in the art which has survived from it. From such survivals the past can be reconstituted and enjoyed. As the quotation from Carlyle at the head of this chapter also suggests, even the future might be predicted.

The idea of reconstruction of the past from the present is one which these writers share with the scientists whose approach constitutes the second strand in the nineteenth-century concern with the relationship of past to present. For them too the decoding of remains – rocks, animals, birds, insects, plants and languages – could provide a method of reconstructing the past which had formed them, though the links could not be made by human memory. Not surprisingly, in geological and evolutionary studies the metaphor of language, used by Ruskin when he speaks of nations writing their 'autobiographies', is dominant. In fact the study of languages on scientific lines was already well developed by the second decade of the century, before Lyell or Darwin wrote. Since many of the early researchers were German or Scandinavian, much of the work was on Germanic languages. Jacob Grimm (1785–1863) examined and reconstructed the relationships between them using whatever documents survived from the seventh to eleventh centuries. Franz Bopp (1791–1837) did comparative work on Sanskrit and Latin as well as Germanic languages. Genealogical trees resembling family trees could be constructed and a common ancestor hypothesized. There was also some discussion of the origins of human language itself and its connections with systems of animal communication. Language studies, like other sciences, worked to show connections between past and present and the process of changing from one to the other: from current forms the earlier equivalences could be determined; past histories and etymologies were thought to shed light on current forms and meanings.

Since all disciplines are capable of translation into the common medium of language, and since spoken or written language had been always self-evidently a transcription from one into the other, it was an obvious metaphor to figure other disciplines. Soon of course, the traffic became two-way with geological and evolutionary terms used metaphorically of language. But the figure of deciphering a language was the most common semiotic which sustained the belief in the past as profoundly significant.

Charles Lyell in *The Principles of Geology* (1830–33) writes in conclusion to his account of 'Methods of Theorizing in Geology': 'These topics we regard as constituting the *alphabet* and *grammar* of geology' (Secord 1997: 356; my emphases). Charles Darwin in *The Origin of Species* (1859) sees himself as 'following Lyell's metaphor' when he looks at the natural geological record 'as a history of the world imperfectly kept and *written in a changing dialect*; of this history we possess the last volume alone, relating only to two or three centuries' (Beer 1996: 251; my emphasis). The task of decoding is seen as difficult: the texts are ambiguous. Some geologists read what was written in the language of rocks as indicating catastrophic upheavals in the past (catastrophe theory). Later, others read it as showing a gradual process of change over long periods of time (uniformitarianism). And critics argue as to whether the flood in *The Mill* indicates adherence to one or the other view. Many of Darwin's predecessors decoded the significance of different species as inscribing a history in which they had preserved an identity given to them by a divine Creator. Darwin (and Alfred Wallace) read it as showing a process in which distinct species had developed through random variations in individuals, some of which chanced to be favoured for survival by the prevailing environment, whilst disfavoured forms became extinct.

Eliot, in writing *The Mill*, engages with the ideas of both scientists and romanticists on the past of society and of individuals. In one aspect her approach is presented as rigorous, like that of Lyell and Darwin; in another it is intuitive and emotionally charged like that of biographical accounts of childhood. The first perspective is captured by Lyell's words at the opening of *The Principles* which might well have come from Eliot:

> By these researches into the state of the earth and its inhabitants at former periods ... we acquire more comprehensive views concerning the laws *now* governing its animate and inanimate productions. When we study history we obtain a more profound insight into human nature, by instituting a comparison between the present and former states of society. (Secord 1997: 5)

In her novel Eliot achieves the appearance of interpreting the present state of the human condition from knowledge of the past which does not need to be hypothesized. She effects this in a handful of long descriptive passages in the authoritative present tense about the past and in many shorter generalizations about human behaviour throughout the narrative.

Three central passages using the present tense all relate to St Ogg's and create a general frame of reference for the text as to the explanatory nature of past history. The first is the opening description of the town in its natural setting, seen on a 'leafless' February afternoon. It parallels the account of fog over London and Chancery at the beginning of *Bleak House*. It is similarly wide-ranging over a fluctuating scene, moving across 'A wide plain, where the broadening Floss hurries on between its green banks to the sea', and panning up the tributary Ripple to Dorlcote Mill. The narrator is placed as a contemporary observer of the scene as it progresses, as though he or she were giving a running commentary on an unfolding event *now*: a waggoner urges on his horses, a small girl watches the millwheel sending up diamond jets of water causing her dog to leap and bark jealously.

Then, in a transition at once shocking and natural, place and time change:

> It is time the little playfellow went in, I think, ... It is time, too, for me to leave off resting my arms on the cold stone of this bridge ...
>
> Ah, my arms are really benumbed. I have been pressing my elbows on the arms of my chair, and dreaming that I was standing on the bridge in front of Dorlcote Mill, as it looked one February afternoon many years ago. Before I dozed off, I was going to tell you what Mr and Mrs Tulliver were talking about, as they sat by the bright fire in the left-hand parlour, on that very afternoon I have been dreaming of. (p. 8)

Then the narrator moves into the narrowing past tense – "'What I want, you know," said Mr Tulliver – "what I want is to give Tom a good eddication"' (p. 8).

With this change what seemed to be the present has dissolved into a distant past, now remembered. This accounts for the narrator's original sense of poignancy at observing an otherwise mundane scene. The change also figures the structure of the whole narrative in which a story of past lives is overlaid by a grid of present tense statements drawn from characters within the text but offered as omnetemporally true. This effect is enhanced by the changed status of the narrator, who appeared at first to be a contemporaneous figure in the scene being described, but is now revealed as a distant and authoritative individual. He or she is also slightly mysterious: the reader cannot place him or her. There emerges the possibility that 'she' is an older version of the small girl (Maggie Tulliver) recounting her own story. But this is later ruled out by references such as that to the 'firmer texture of our youth and manhood' (p. 57) which make clear a male identity, as well as, eventually, by Maggie's death. This leaves the narrator as an anonymous, knowing figure who can move freely between present and past, and who is shown to understand the laws of existence. He is the equivalent not of one or other of the narrators in *Bleak House* but of both.

The next long passage of this kind reverts to St Ogg's and to the present tense later in Book One:

> It is one of those old, old towns which impress one as a continuation and outgrowth of nature, as much as the nets of the bower-birds or the winding galleries of the white ants: a town which carries the

traces of its long growth and history like a millennial tree, and has
sprung up and developed in the same spot between the river and the
low hill from the time when the Roman legions turned their backs
on it ... (p. 101)

What follows is a past-tense summary of St Ogg's history from Roman
times onwards evoked by the tumulus, 'fine old hall' and 'Gothic fa-
cade and towers', as well as by the river and the landscape, from which
the narrator decodes the past and gives it a permanent and
omnetemporal value. The passage also functions to fill out the framework of reference for the narrative. It does this by literally seeing the
town as an outgrowth of nature, one more aspect of a human environment in which landscape, buildings, artefacts, animals and people constitute a seamless whole. Like the geological past and that of plants and
animals, the human past is given a priority over present existence.

Such a framework is expressive of what Eliot, in a discursive piece
on the work of the German writer Wilhelm, Heinrich von Riehl (1823–
97), refers to in the opening phrase of her title 'The Natural History of
German Life'. This description of Riehl's *Die bürgerliche Geschellschaft*
is explained by Eliot's paraphrase of his views:

> The external conditions which society has inherited from the past
> are but the manifestation of inherited internal conditions in the hu-
> man beings who compose it; the internal and the external are related
> to each other as the organism and its medium, and development can
> take place only by the consentaneous development of both. (Byatt
> and Warren 1990: 127)

This is 'natural history' in Darwin's sense of the interaction of organism
and environment and it is the essence of how past and present are seen
to relate: it takes society to be part of the wider natural environment
that surrounds all living creatures, and it makes absolutely clear that
for development to take place organisms and their surroundings must
interact. This is a crucial aspect of the general theoretical framework
within which the narrative operates, and the location for the treatment
of human (and social) growth. Like the rest of living creatures, human
beings are designed to grow and develop. That is why *The Mill* is so
often described as a *Bildungsroman*, remarkable in that it shows the
shaping of a woman not a man.

In another significant passage which opens Book Four of the narrative, the present tense again signals an authoritative account in which
the crucial integration of St Ogg's and its surrounding landscape is
reiterated. Here the geographical picture spreads to include ruined towns
on the River Rhône as compared with superb castles on the River Rhine.
While the castles have 'a natural fitness' to grow out of the 'green and
rocky steeps', the Rhône towns are 'dismal remnants of commonplace
houses' signalling a 'narrow, ugly and grovelling existence' endured until they were 'swept into the same oblivion with the generations of ants
and beavers' (p. 237) as perhaps 'the emmet-like' Dodsons and Tullivers
may be. Thus the recognition of a universe in which humanity is part
of the natural world, in these three focal passages referring to St Ogg's,
becomes available as a point of reference throughout the text. Through
their use of the present tense the narrator is able to announce
omnetemporal truths which apply both to nature's creatures and to
humanity.

For instance, Tulliver's reaction to the loss of his law-suit against
Wakem and the financial ruin it causes him is the occasion for one of a
web of such brief present-tense generalizations. The man shifts rapidly
from a determination not to be under an obligation to anyone, to a
confidence that his wife will easily be able to borrow the necessary money
from her parsimonious brother-in-law, Pullet. This spurious belief is
presented as the operation of a law familiar in nature: 'There are certain animals … [that] … can never flourish again after a single wrench:
and there are certain human beings to whom predominance is a law of
life – they can only sustain humiliation so long as they can refuse to
believe in it, and, in their own conception predominate still' (p. 173).
The lawyer, Riley's, willingness to put work in the way of a stupid clergyman is ironically justified by the argument that 'Nature herself occasionally quarters an inconvenient parasite on an animal towards whom
she has otherwise no ill-will' (p. 23). Tulliver is the animal, Stelling
merely the inconvenient parasite. Stelling himself is said to be 'an animal under the immediate teaching of nature': He therefore imitates, in
his inflexible application of a single teaching method to all comers 'like
Mr Broderip's amiable beaver' which that naturalist records in 1852,
acting as nature taught it to build, built a dam 'in a room up three
pairs of stairs in London' out of brooms, warming pans, sticks, boots,

clothes, coal, etc, (p. 121). He has no more understanding of how difficult education is than 'an animal endowed with a power of boring
through a rock should be expected to have wide views of excavation' (p.
147). Tom under this regime shares the 'blank unimaginativeness concerning the cause of his sufferings' of 'an innocent shrew-mouse imprisoned in one split trunk in an ash tree' (p. 123). Tom is an excellent
and stupid lad who runs at obstacles 'in a truly ingenuous bovine manner' (p. 155). Later it is asserted that to suppose Waken to have 'the
same sort of inveterate hatred towards Tulliver, that Tulliver had towards him, would be like supposing that a pike and a roach can look at
each other from a similar point of view' (p. 219). And it is noted that
the spiritual seed scattered over Tulliver is sadly destitute of those hooks
which nature has supplied to certain seeds that 'are required to find a
nidus for themselves under unfavourable circumstances'. Consequently
he sees a distinction between religion and common sense (p. 240).

By implication the narrator has a perfect grasp of these universal
laws and articulates them as omnetemporally true. This means that
Carlyle's comment on time in *Past and Present* (1843) might refer equally
to the present tense as Eliot uses it in *The Mill*: 'the Present holds in it
both the whole Past and whole Future' (Altick 1977: 42). As Carlyle
implies, future time is latent in the present. Similarly these
omnetemporal generalizations are predictions of their own future truth.
They also re-emphasize the relatedness of all creation in a way achieved
by Darwin by a similarly specific comment at the end of *The Origin of
Species*. Surveying an 'entangled bank' inhabited by plants, birds, insects and worms, he claims that there is 'a grandeur in this view of life'
on account of the fact that 'these elaborately constructed forms, so
different from each other, and dependent on each other in so complex
a manner have all been produced by laws acting around us' (Beer 1996:
395).

But the account of the past in Eliot's text is more complex than is
suggested by the scientific framework which inhabits it. The use of the
present tense – the tense of what is true at all times – gives moral authority to the values of the past. Such authority, however, works against
the grain of other elements in the text which define the past as stasis,
and change as the only hope for a wider life. That framework is about
adaptation, growth, development and decay. It is destabilized by the

treatment of the past of individuals. From the retrospective viewpoint established at the end of the first short chapter, the lives of Maggie and Tom are charged with an emotional nostalgia that is Wordsworthian, in that it is based on intuition rather than logic. Like Maggie Tulliver, Darwin and Ruskin in their autobiographies, as already demonstrated, exemplify a nineteenth-century tendency to represent childhood as idyllic. Yet Darwin lost his mother at the age of eight and Ruskin endured 'ceaseless authority' and surveillance which left him, as he says, 'cramped indeed, but not disciplined' (Cockshut 1994: 32). Like them, Maggie Tulliver endures much pain as a child. She suffers anguish through her vulnerability to Tom's displeasure over trivial offences such as forgetting to feed his rabbits; through her relatives' disparaging comments on her appearance and temperament as compared with those of her doll-like cousin Lucy; and through a prevailing view that her intellectual talents are necessarily superficial and, anyway, inappropriate in a female. Better for a man, as Maggie's father points out, to make the choice of a wife depend on finding (as he did) someone more stupid than himself. The extremity of Maggie's distress is figured by her brutal treatment of the Fetish-doll 'which she punished for all her misfortunes'. 'Three nails driven into the head' commemorate 'as many crises in Maggie's nine years of earthly struggle' (p. 25). Characteristically, this way of expressing feeling (along with beating the Fetish's head against the wall) has been suggested by her reading. She has found the story in the Bible of Jael destroying Sisera and drawn upon the illustration to it. Yet these facts do not inhibit the narrator's authoritative assertion of the paradisal nature of this time in her life any more than Darwin's or Ruskin's real experiences do.

Paradise is an image used by him when Maggie's and Tom's lives change for the worse after their father's ruin. Significantly it is Paradise lost. Their state is equated with Adam and Eve's expulsion from the Garden of Eden: 'They had entered the thorny wilderness, and the golden gates of their childhood had for ever closed behind them' (p. 168). But this paradise, strangely, is sealed over for ever in an unchanging state. This retrospectively happy childhood is claimed to be a source of all later joy and knowledge. Yet the past is not a point of growth but an uncrossable frontier: it is eternally shut off and incapable of alteration. It is marked by an absence of choice and, significantly, an inability to

distinguish the self from the outer world, that crucial precondition for
the interaction between the two needed, as Eliot claims in the essay on
Riehl, for individual and social development. Its frozen joy, like that of
Keats's urn, is sterile in terms of later human happiness.

The same sleight of hand in the manipulation of tense is evident
here as in the opening of the novel. There is an equivocation in 'the
same flowers come up again every spring … the same hips and haws …
the same redbreasts' which would be removed if the word 'same' were
dropped. The recurrent cycle of the seasons is a fact, the sameness of
the flowers a fancy. It is a metaphorical generalization. Its conclusion
lacks conviction more markedly in a period which, like ours, is ad-
dicted to the notion of unhappy childhoods. Even in Eliot's own time
it can scarcely have been accepted that the universal answer to the narrator's rhetorical question is 'None' when he asks: 'What novelty is worth
that sweet monotony where everything is known, and *loved* because it
is known' (p. 36). The eulogy becomes a hymn to stasis.

Similarly, childhood is even said to lay down the prototype of all
subsequent experience of happiness:

> Our delight in the sunshine on the deep-bladed grass today, might
> be no more than the faint perception of wearied souls, if it were not
> for the sunshine and the grass in the far-off years which still live in
> us, and transform our perception into love.

The nature of a static past is shown to set limits to future happiness:

> We could never have loved the earth so well if we had had no child-
> hood in it, – if it were not the earth where the same flowers come up
> every spring that we used to gather with our tiny fingers as we sat
> lisping to ourselves on the grass – the same hips and haws on the
> autumn hedgerows – the same redbreasts that we used to call 'God's
> birds' because they did no harm to the precious crops. (p. 36)

Childhood is assumed to be the only source from which humanity can
learn 'the mother tongue of our imagination, the language that is laden
with all the subtle inextricable associations, the fleeting hours of childhood left behind them' (p. 36). Adult life as an imperfect memory of
childhood comes close to Wordsworth's 'Ode on the Intimation of
Immortality from Recollection of Early Childhood':

> O Joy! that in our embers
> Is something that doth live,
> That nature yet remembers
> What was so fugitive!
> The thought of our past years in me doth breed
> Perpetual benediction.
>
> (ll. 133–8)

In *The Mill* these early experiences are shown as an appropriate source of moral values in adult life, curbing self-interest and ambition, 'That striving' to which we might succumb 'if the loves and sanctities of our life had no deep immoveable root in memory'. The past is the unchangeable measure of both joy and right conduct.

There is a discrepancy in the novel between the recurrent idea (expressed in the long passages referred to earlier) that phylogeny and ontogeny run in parallel and the working out of individual destiny in the text. At the opening of Book Four with its account of contrasting societies it has been made clear that societies like St Ogg's which cling mindlessly to 'hereditary custom' will decay, not grow. Only those individuals who question this clinging to the past in changing times offer the potential for development by reacting to such change so that 'gradual consentaneous development' of society and individuals can take place (Byatt and Warren 1990: 127). Maggie and Tom (who illogically is always lumped together with her) are offered in Book Four as examples of how the oppressive narrowness affects those 'young natures that in the onward tendency of human things have risen above the mental level of the generation before them, to which they have been nevertheless tied by the strongest fibres of their hearts' (p. 238). But when Maggie's progress is plotted as to the struggle between her breadth of vision and her attachments to family, she can be seen to cling to the past in a way which is paradoxically represented as the means of preserving her moral integrity. The contradictory views that development means intelligent and considered reaction to circumstance, and that morality consists in maintaining the values of a previous generation, are both given the status of omnetemporal truths on a par with 'man is mortal'.

The paradox in the treatment of society and the individual builds into the narratives precisely the dilemma that confronts Maggie in her dealings with her two suitors, Philip Wakem and Stephen Guest. When she meets Philip as an adult she has already turned to a voice from the past, in the shape of Thomas à Kempis's book on *The Imitation of Christ*, to deal with her joyless existence after her father's ruin. It is a life composed of 'little sordid tasks' and 'weary joyless leisure' (p. 250), with an unhappy father, a wretched mother and a brother bent on revenge. All this is made worse by what she assumes to be an illicit 'wide hopeless yearning for something, whatever it was, that was greatest and best' (p. 252). The 'revelatory' solution that à Kempis provides fits perfectly the ideal of womanliness around her: the practice of 'renunciation', 'self-humiliation and entire devotedness' (p. 24) – the values of the past.

Then the external, the 'medium', impinges on 'the organism' that is Maggie when Philip offers her some of the things she has longed for hopelessly.

> Here suddenly was an opening in the rocky wall which shut in the narrow valley of humiliation, where all her prospect was the remote unfathomed sky; and some of the memory-haunting earthly delights were no longer out of her reach. She might have books, converse, affection – she might hear tidings of the world from which her mind had not yet lost its sense of exile. (pp. 285–6)

Eventually, at Tom's bidding, she has to choose between this and her old path of renunciation. His reason for insisting that she should break with Philip is past history: his father's command that he should carry on the feud with Philip's father which resulted in the disastrous lawsuit, the loss of the Tulliver money and of the mill. The past is captured in the oath never to forgive Waken that Tom wrote into the family bible. This inscription, like that other writing from the past by à Kempis, demands the renunciation of individual choice and of change. Maggie chooses the past, rather than Philip and the new extended life he offers, but with some equivocation. She reverts to penitence and submission but finds them 'obstructed by resentment that would present itself to her no otherwise than as just indignation' (p. 306).

The second encounter with a man who offers Maggie a future which will release her from 'oppressive narrowness', the 'narrow valley' of her childhood past, ends less equivocally. It is represented as an extreme betrayal of her past and a strong temptation to choose a different life, one that is deeply attractive to her as an individual. By agreeing to elope with the irresistible Stephen Guest, her cousin Lucy's fiancé, she would simultaneously break with the moral code of the Dodsons and Tullivers and betray a trusted friend and relative. This would be a choice based on personal desire. The nature of the temptation is figured in a surrogate seduction scene which contemporary reviewers read as such and which they found disgusting.

Maggie lets herself drift dreamily along in a small boat rowed by Stephen until they have gone too far to turn back. The narrator, in present tense and generalizing mode, half endorses her passivity: 'All yielding is attended with a less vivid consciousness than insistence; it is the partial sleep of thought'. The motion of the boat, her weariness and exhaustion and her 'fatigued sensations' equate with her 'complete subjection to that strong mysterious charm which made a last parting from Stephen seem the death of all joy' (p. 410). In yielding to the seductions of the moment as they impinge upon an ardent nature stifled by a narrow life, Maggie momentarily abandons the ideal of selflessness. She drinks in the 'nectar' of Stephen's pleas for an elopement with 'thirsty lips', feeling that 'there *must* be, then, a life for mortals here below which was not hard and chill – in which affection would no longer be self-sacrifice' (p. 411).

But the past, and in particular her childhood, has taught Maggie irrevocably that love (for Tom) *always* means self-sacrifice. In a chapter called 'Waking', she awakes to this old 'unchangeable' truth in which 'faithfulness and constancy' equate with 'renouncing whatever is opposed to the reliance others have in us' (p. 417). In an equivocal but generalizing metaphor her past life is described as 'grasping her in this way, in a tightening clutch which comes in the last moments of possible rescue' (pp. 413–14). It is uncertain whether the past is the means of rescue or what she needs to be rescued from. Whichever it is, the power of the past succeeds in holding her, temporarily seeming to be the 'clue of life', the thread which leads her out of the maze of moral confusion. In what is often seen as the pivotal point of her life and of the text, Maggie asks Stephen desperately 'If the past is not to bind us, where can duty lie?' (p. 417). This fulcrum of the narrative is a purely rhetorical question implying its own answer: that the past *is* where duty lies. With this her dilemma is reduced to one for which this true-at-all-times-and-in-all-circumstances maxim provides a certain answer. The answer is not consonant, however, with the childhood narrative that has shown in detail the inadequacies of a society fittingly described as a 'narrow valley' surrounded by a 'rocky wall' within which familiar norms of appearance, behaviour and abilities are the only ones acceptable for any female, regardless of the individual.

Those reviewers not too shocked by Maggie's ability merely to feel temptation praised this choice of renunciation as moral strength. The contemporary acceptance of her choice as noble is echoed by the narrator's admiring attitude to a decision which causes Maggie great anguish and also, tellingly, self-reproach. She is represented as longing for a punitive reaction from her brother which would be appropriate to her situation. This presumably is because the mere temptation is seen as a terrible weakness. Again this is an attitude reflected in the reviews. A typical comment is 'The *indulgence* of such a sentiment for the affianced of a friend under whose roof she was, was a treachery and a meanness ... and nothing can afterwards lift the character into the same hold on us. The refusal to marry Stephen fails to do so' (Carroll 1971: 121). The narrator comments approvingly on Maggie's self-flagellation as indicative of a terrible struggle; and as one reviewer points out, except for 'the one element of overwhelming fascination not one word is uttered in palliation' of her temptation to yield to Stephen (Carroll 1971: 129). Yet by equating duty with the values of her family in her simple rhetorical question Maggie is returning to the view of life held by her brother. He is 'a man of maxims', one of the category of people who have 'minds that are guided in their moral judgements solely by moral rules', without taking the trouble to exert 'patience, discrimination, impartiality' (p. 438). There is a sharp difference between a life governed by these unconsidered rules and the idyllic childhood of pure sensation which in Maggie's imagination illogically validates them.

In accordance with these rules Tom finally judges Maggie in terms of his father's injunction and his own sworn oath – never to forgive the enemy. This has applied to Wakem and his son and, once Maggie has apparently disgraced the family name, to her too. She must *never* be forgiven. The poverty of a life lived according to primitive moral rules as though they had the truth of mathematical axioms has been stressed throughout the narrative by the association of such lives with a narrow literalism. Mr Riley recommends Mr Stelling, of whom he knows nothing, as a teacher because he believes that a man who had a university education could teach anything he liked. Stelling himself sets about teaching with an unvarying 'uniformity of method and independence of circumstances' (p. 121), ignoring any unfortunate consequences. He ascribes to sheer obstinacy Tom's inability to learn Latin or to deal with mathematical abstractions. Tom's uncle Glegg is later shown to be contemptuous of whatever his education has been, on the grounds that 'if it had been good for anything, so successful a man as himself would hardly have been ignorant of it' (p. 200). After the ill-fated law-suit Mrs Tulliver goes in person to ask Wakem not to buy up the mill, in a simple belief that if he sees 'a respectable matron like herself disposed to "give him good words", why shouldn't he listen to her representations?' (p. 215). And she is baffled by her husband's metaphor when he claims that she *would not* want him to hire a good labourer "cause he'd got a mole on his face' (p. 10), because this particular incident has never happened.

It is such literalism that the narrator scrutinizes in the account of Tom's schooling where the used of metaphors as maxims or axioms is attacked. Stelling uses such a hackneyed figure to justify his practice as a teacher of 'one regimen for all minds'. Since Tom's brain seems impervious to etymology and geometry the clergyman assumes that it needs to be 'ploughed and harrowed by these patent implements'. His favourite justificatory metaphor is that the 'classics and geometry constituted that culture of the mind which prepared it for the reception of any subsequent crop' (p 122). The figure is neatly exploded by replacing 'cultivation' with a more idiosyncratic figure, appropriate to the victim of Stelling's efforts. It is pointed out that Tom is affected by the regimen 'as if he had been plied with cheese in order to remedy a gastric weakness which prevented him from digesting it' (p. 123). Other clichéd figures are then piled up to show how ridiculously limited they are:

> Once call the brain an intellectual stomach, and one's ingenious conception of the classics and geometry as ploughs and harrows seems to settle nothing. But then it is open to someone else to follow great authorities, and call the mind a sheet of white paper or a mirror, in which case one's knowledge of the digestive process becomes quite irrelevant. It was doubtless an ingenious idea to call a camel the ship

of the desert, but it would hardly lead one far in training that useful beast. (p. 123)

What is at issue here is not stylistic taste nor the subject of metaphor itself. As Rignall in relation to another passage says, 'The contrast between narrow-minded Tom and large-souled Maggie is, among other things, a contrast between different forms of knowledge' as well as 'different ways of using language' (Rignall 1993: 36). Tom is characterized throughout the narrative as one of those to whom 'prejudices come as the natural food of tendencies which can get no sustenance out of that complex, fragmentary, doubt-provoking knowledge which we call truth' (p. 400). This is a description of the Dodsons, Tullivers and their like in St Ogg's which reappears in various comments throughout the text. Even under 'the iron hand of misfortune', they show little trace of religion and 'their moral notions though held with strong tenacity, seem to have no standard beyond hereditary custom' (p. 238). The narrator then employs a skilfully manipulative use of the pronoun 'you' to impose this view: 'You could not live among such people: you are stifled for the want of an outlet towards something beautiful great and noble'. Then the coercion is at once softened and enforced as he locates himself among his stifled readers: 'I share with you this sense of oppressive narrowness; but it is necessary that we should feel it, if we care to understand …' (p. 238). This is reiterated after Maggie's last renunciation in a directly admonitory address: 'our life is not to be embraced by maxims, and … to lace ourselves up in formulas of that sort is to repress all the divine promptings and inspirations that spring from growing insight and sympathy' (p. 438). An even broader generalization is drawn from this when the narrator asserts that 'The great problem of the shifting relation between passion and duty is clear to no man who is capable of apprehending it' (p. 437).

At an earlier place in the text Maggie and Tom are seen as potential growth points. They have risen above the 'mental level' of the previous generation though remain emotionally attached to it. Or so it is said, though Tom's rise is never evident. Maggie, however, does struggle to translate her belief that there are wider horizons and better things to be sought for, into some kind of development in her life. On a chain of guilt like a bear tied to a post, she reverts repeatedly to renouncing what she wants. In effect she has learnt a new language from what she read and from her friendship with Philip Wakem. As an out-sider from the masculine world on account of his physique, he was able to offer her a new emotional literacy which sets up an opposition to the idea that being bound by the past is morally noble. Unlike Tom, he was comfortable in dealing with abstractions and could speak of emotions in a way unfamiliar to Maggie. He countered her talk of renunciation of a way of life by seeing it as the death of feeling and of the finer self: 'It seems to me we can never give up longing and wishing while we are thoroughly alive. There are certain things we feel to be beautiful and good, and we *must* hunger after them. How can we ever be satisfied without them until our feelings are deadened' (p. 266). Music for instance, he says, can change his attitude of mind and make him feel capable of heroism.

This is the language that Maggie needs to express herself, and it is the kind for which Eliot shows a passionate preference in her essay on Riehl's work. It is a form with 'whims of idiom', 'cumbrous forms', a 'fitful shimmer of many-hued significance', even 'hoary archaisms' – 'everything that gives it power to express the imagination and to com-pel it. Only such a form as this will serve to express *life*, which is a great deal more than science'. Science unlike '*life*' can be served by a 'patent, deodorized and nonresonant language' which effects communication as precisely and unambiguously as 'algebraic signs'. Like Maggie, Eliot in her essay recognizes that 'one word stands for many things, and many words for one thing' while 'the subtle shades of meaning, and still sub-tler echoes of association' make language into a powerful instrument. It must be left 'to grow in precision, completeness, and unity, as minds grow in clearness, comprehensiveness, and sympathy' (Byatt and War-ren 1990: 128). Here as elsewhere the parallels are implied between the development of language, individuals and society.

In embracing an all-purpose maxim as the deciding factor in her decision about Stephen, Maggie is rejecting the language and way of life that Philip taught her and re-embracing a sterile past as a moral touchstone. She does this in order to revert compulsively to the à Kempis doctrine of renunciation as the right way of life. When reading *Imitation of Christ* she forms plans for 'self-humiliation and entire devotedness … renunciation seemed to her the entrance into that satisfaction she had so long been craving in vain' (p. 254). This is merely an earlier version of Ruskin's insistence in 'Of Queens' Gardens' (1865) that 'Women' at least must be 'incorruptibly good, … instinctively, infallibly wise – wise, not for self development … but for self-renunciation' (Helsinger, Sheets and Veeder 1983: 1.82). In the encounter later with Stephen, Eliot's difficulty is a usual one for those who questioned nineteenth-century stereotypes of femininity: how to contest the idea that selflessness is an essentially 'feminine' characteristic without denigrating women or self-sacrifice. It is a particular difficulty to her because altruism is the centre of her morality. To an extent she deals with the problem by showing and admiring this quality in Philip too but, as will appear later, this fails to resolve the difficulty.

Maggie's selfless decision to leave Stephen because her past requires it appears to some degree a self-punishment, because her rejection of him comes too late to avoid damaging Lucy and Philip. It merely damages irreparably her own reputation and future life in St Ogg's. As one female critic says, she found the 'chief perplexity' of this episode to be in the fact that 'we feel that, granting the case as our author puts it, the mischief done, the mutual passion mutually confessed, Stephen's piteous arguments have some justice on their side. The wrong done to him in Maggie's forsaking him was almost as great as the wrong previously done to Philip and Lucy:– whom no self sacrifice on her part or Stephen's could ever have made happy again' (Carroll 1971: 159). Her decision in this light is merely self-flagellation.

Some recent critics have tried to deal with the encoding of this reactionary view of self-abnegation as essential for women by arguing that contradictory accounts of Maggie and her aspirations are somehow balanced. Contemporary reviewers did not read the text in this way. They frequently found it awkwardly disjointed and complain that the parts of it do not fit together. The general unease is summed up in the *Guardian*'s rebuke: 'We do not expect, and it is hardly pleasant, to be called in the same work from one set of thoughts, and, still more, one set of feelings, to another; to have them suddenly strained and screwed up' (Carroll 1971: 130). Another review concludes that 'uncertainty is the prevailing impression with which we close *The Mill on the Floss*' (Carroll 1971: 159). This is true not only because these wavering views of femininity and of the importance of female individuality disrupt the treatment of Maggie, but also because of the consequent effects on the portrayal of masculinity. This is inevitable at a time when gender identity is commonly constructed on the basic acceptance of the complementary nature of femininity and masculinity. Lucy and Maggie clearly figure the stereotypical feminine and the critique of it with all the contradictions this entails. Masculinity, as represented by Tom Tulliver, Philip Wakem and Stephen Guest, is an even more elusive concept. As already pointed out in chapter 2, the defensive term current for those assumed to approximate to the masculine ideal was the approving adjective 'manly'. Each of the three men is assessed (uncertainly) in relation to a 'manliness' marked by physical robustness and handsomeness, as well as directness, clear-headedness and also chivalry towards 'the weaker sex'. Such a construct is based, as Sussman points out, on a definition of 'manliness' as the control and discipline of a dangerous 'maleness' fantasized as 'potent yet dangerous energy' (Sussman 1995: 13). Of the three only Philip is not dangerous.

The narrative in the first two Books, 'Boy and Girl' and 'School-time', is structured around the asymmetrical relationship between sister and brother: Maggie is carefully shown to exceed or deviate from the expectations of what a proper girl is like. This is effected by showing that she surpasses her male sibling in intelligence, breadth of mind, sensitivity, capacity for feeling and insight. (There is also the subordinate contrast with pretty stereotypical Lucy.) The spectrum of complementary characteristics is redivided in this account, leaving Tom lacking what Maggie possesses. This makes the narratorial generalizations about the two which treat their experience as homogeneous, baffling to the reader. Contemporary reviews certainly read Tom as defective. They comment characteristically that he has 'a narrow solid mind' with 'not much depth or variety' (Carroll 1971: 110); 'that he is chiefly remarkable for self-assertion and hard headed resistance to fate', as well as 'harsh justice and stinging disregard'; and he is 'self-confiding, narrow, inexorable and inconsiderate' (Carroll 1971: 128). Yet when he is humiliated, as Maggie so often is, by Mr Stelling's crude teaching methods, his suffering is portrayed as feminine: 'under this vigorous treatment Tom became more like a girl than he had ever been in his life before' (p. 124).

Yet paradoxically because he is the object of Maggie's passionate affection and her love for him must be seen as appropriate, Tom is not subject to narratorial contempt. Eliot herself claimed not to express distaste for him when a critic assumed she did (Carroll 1971: 137). Instead his decisiveness and obstinacy are several times approved of as 'manly'. His family recognizes 'manliness' (p. 187) in his tone when after his father's downfall he asks Aunt Glegg for a loan to buy back his mother's furniture at the bankruptcy sale. His single-mindedness (or narrow-mindedness) in pursuing his task of paying off the debts is translated into a central virtue that is said to give him the essential quality for manliness. Significantly, Maggie is said to lack this 'prudence and self-command which were the qualities that made Tom manly in the midst of his intellectual boyishness' (p. 241). The self-command referred to is supposed to control his dangerous qualities. But this attempt to redress the balance is defeated by the lack of chivalrous protectiveness to Maggie that 'manliness' requires. A weak and extraneous example of this quality is devised in the form of his kindness to the infant Laura Stelling when he is appropriated as a babysitter. If he had had a worse disposition, it is said, he would have hated her 'but he had too much in him of the fibre that turns to true manliness, and to protecting pity for the weak' (p. 126).

This isolated incident serves only to underline the lack of such a feeling in relation not only to Maggie, but also to Philip for whom he is a reciprocal point of reference. Philip is set up in many ways as the opposite of Tom: the present who can offer Maggie things her past and her brother cannot give. He is cleverer and far better educated than Tom, closer to Maggie and women generally in his possession of intellectual curiosity, imagination and susceptibility to emotion. *His* attitude to Maggie is always chivalrous: kind, understanding and protective. But these qualities do not cause the narrator to characterize him as 'manly': he is not holding down 'potentially destructive male energy' (Sussman 1995: 25). He is more readily turned into someone who becomes a butt for what others see as unmanliness. Tom's immediate judgement of him when he appears at Stelling's is that his hair waves and curls 'like a girl's' and that he is a 'pale puny fellow' and would not be able 'to play at anything worth speaking of' (p. 142). Predictably, when they quarrel, the abuse Tom throws at him is that he is unmanly (though the term is not used): 'You know I won't hit you, because you're no better than a girl' (p. 152). Philip's gifts, those qualities that enable him to offer an escape from her 'rocky valley' are to a large extent the result of his deformity which has caused him to devote himself 'like a girl' not to 'masculine' pursuits but to reading, drawing, music. Both he and Maggie see the reference to his physique as 'unmanly' and say so to Tom. The narrator seems unable to detach the idea of femininity from the very qualities that he admires in Philip. He half suggests feelings of distaste:

> Kept aloof from all practical life as Philip had been, and by nature half feminine in sensitiveness, he had some of the woman's intolerant repulsion towards worldliness and the deliberate pursuit of sensual enjoyment ... Perhaps there is inevitably something morbid in a human being who is in any way unfavourably excepted from ordinary conditions ... (p. 291)

Fatally, this is echoed by Maggie's reaction to her enforced break with him at Tom's insistence. Despite her pain and anger towards Tom for believing Philip unworthy not only because he is Wakem's son, but also because he is deformed, she is aware of 'a certain dim background of relief' at the enforced separation. The episode ends with a question ambiguous in itself and also as to whether it is Maggie or the narrator's thought: 'Surely it was only because the sense of a deliverance from concealment was welcome at any cost' (p. 306).

The insinuation that Maggie feels that Philip's unthreatening deformity and physical feebleness, and intellectual and artistic pursuits make him effeminate or unmanly becomes stronger in the episode with Stephen. This seems to show that a handsome and strong physique is a manifestation of 'manliness'. Particularly significant is the narrator's comment when Stephen offers Maggie his arm: 'There is something strangely winning to most women in that offer of the firm arm: the help is not wanted physically at that moment, but the sense of help – the presence of strength that is outside them and yet theirs – meets a continual want of the imagination' (p. 358). Apart from this, Stephen is characterized, as women frequently are in nineteenth-century narrative, by his appearance and demeanour. This starts with satirical references to his diamond ring, attar of roses and air of nonchalance which are the incongruously 'graceful and odiferous result of the largest oil-mill and the most extensive wharf in St Ogg's' (p. 319). But the satire fades and he is described with unaffected admiration for his 'square forehead, short dark-brown hair standing erect, with a slight wave at the end, like a thick crop of corn, and a half-ardent, half-sarcastic glance from under his well-marked horizontal eye-brows' (p. 320). This sentimentalized, pseudo-Byronic appearance, however, seems to turn him into a physically appropriate husband for Maggie, particularly when a beautiful bass voice and willingness to give up all for love, are added. Throughout the scenes of his gradual involvement with Maggie there is a noticeable absence of judgemental comment. It is overpowering passion and the pain that rejection causes which are insisted upon. He is a hollow individual who would surely figure low in the manliness stakes but the question is evaded, or rather scotched, though the structuring of the text would suggest it. Maggie momentarily suggests it by accusing him of unmanliness in not telling her how far the boat has come – 'You have wanted to deprive me of any choice. You knew we were come too far – you have dared to take advantage of my thoughtlessness. It is unmanly to bring me into such a position' (p. 409). He is able quickly to disarm her by admitting his guilt. From this point neither she nor the narrator judges him.

This fact struck contemporary reviewers, familiar with what constituted manliness, they were ready to judge him as lacking it: 'the hero (sic) escapes with but a qualified reprobation: his dishonourable abduction of Maggie is treated as the quite natural result of his passion for her'. This reviewer even adds tartly that 'in George Eliot's eyes he is not disgraced by conduct that would cause any honourable man to turn his back on him'. This is 'the result of that fascination when men exercise over women ... and affords a cardinal test and patent demonstration, if it were still needed, of George Eliot's sex' (Carroll 1971: 141). None of the three men achieves 'manliness' but there is no doubt which one is most magnanimously treated by the narrator.

What this review indicates is a contemporary male reaction: that his seduction of Maggie is despicably unmanly. Swinburne makes the same judgement in surprisingly blimpish terms: 'the man ... does not exist who would make for the first time the acquaintance of Mr. Stephen Guest with no incipient sense of a twitching in his fingers, and a tingling in his toes at the notion of any contact between Maggie Tulliver and a cur so far beneath the chance of promotion to the notice of his horsewhip, or elevation to the level of his boot' (Carroll 1971: 165). All three men who figure as partners to Maggie are represented in ways determined by the fact that she is an exceptional and unstereotypical woman.

The uncertainty of the text has always been most clearly seen in relation to the death of the Tullivers in the flood. Boumelha, in a perceptive essay, summarizes some of the ways it has been read or been explained away as 'a revenge murder of Tom; a narrator's murder of Maggie; the destruction of the restrictive community; the fulfilment of incest fantasy' and others. Boumelha herself sees it as a way out of the impasse for 'a woman for whom no meaningful future … can be imagined' (Roe 1987: 29). What an initial focus on past and present tenses shows is that these are ways of spelling out what contemporaries meant by 'a glorious Euthanasia' (Carroll 1971: 158) or an ending in which 'the story is carried off its legs by the flood' (Carroll 1971: 151). It shows that uncertainties and instabilities of the text are captured in the oscillation of tenses which juxtapose contradictory assertions.

4

Gain and loss:
the magic future in *Daniel Deronda*

'Second sight' is a flag over disputed ground. But it is a matter
of knowledge that there are persons whose yearnings,
conceptions – nay, travelled conclusions take the form of images
which have a foreshadowing power. (*Daniel Deronda*, chapter
38)

THE preoccupation with the past that Eliot reveals in *The Mill on
the Floss* gives way in *Daniel Deronda* (1876) to a concern with
what is to come. Unlike the earlier novel, which blocks off a future by
drowning the two central characters, *Daniel Deronda* concerns itself
crucially with contrasting views of what the 'disputed ground' of the
future will bring. The early part of the narrative focuses on individual
expectations while the latter part transfers attention to the broad issue
of the future of the Jewish race, or rather, as Bryan Cheyette sees it in
his *Constructions of 'the Jew' in English Literature and Society 1875–1945*
(1993), the English race as transformed by Jewish aspirations to nationhood. Long before F. R. Leavis dismissed the Jewish section as weak
and irrelevant, some contemporary critics took the view that 'The Judaic
element comes second in the book – the human element comes first'
(Carroll 1971: 471). Others disagreed and even in 1877 David
Kaufmann in *George Eliot and Judaism* claimed that 'The two narratives are to be regarded as pendant, mutually illustrating and explaining one another' (p. 49).

This view is one that recent critics have developed. In doing so they
have heeded George Eliot's own assertion, 'I meant everything in the
book to be related to everything else there' (Haight 1954–68: 6: 290).

But they have continued to find these elements in the text, both human and national, conflicting or even incompatible. The conflict relates to differing projections of the future linked by ideas of 'gain and loss' which thread through the narrative as does the phrase itself. In projecting what the future will hold, the thinker is always in one sense or another focusing on one or both of these issues, 'will I (or my race) benefit from this or that course of action that I am now about to take?' This is the question that propels the capitalist society that Eliot represents in her novel. It fuels the conduct of investment, trade, empire and marriage. If the novel has a central issue it is this, though it does not follow that it will necessarily lead to the contradiction–free text that Leavis and others had a taste for. For this reason I propose to consider the text in relation to its treatment of future reference. This first requires a summary of the forms of such reference in English and their potential.

It is likely to be assumed that statements about the future will involve the use of a future tense, as though there were a future tense which, with past and present tenses, serves to provide linguistic equivalents for visual markers on some universal clock. But in traditional grammar 'tense' has a narrow meaning. It tends to be treated as 'an inflexional category of the verb'. In practice, present English deploys not a modification analogous to *drink–drank* or *walk–walked* but a range of periphrastic forms, in particular modal verbs *will* and *shall* (which derive from early verbs meaning 'wish' and 'must'). English has a variety of these analytic forms (*will/shall/would/should* + *verb*, *be* + *verb* + *ing*) or the present tense. So *I will/shall/must etc. go, I am going/go* to London tomorrow. In addition there are non-verbal ways of referring to the future. They include adverbs like *soon*, phrases like *in the next week*, clauses like *when it's closer to Christmas*, or dates like *December 24th*. Commands or directives also come into the category of future reference: '*Let us go then*, you and I ...' As these examples show, it is unusual for anyone to speak of the future without some subjective colouring of hope, expectation, intent, wish or compulsion. Examples without such colouring are likely to refer to timetabling:

> *I am going to London on Friday not Thursday.*
> *The dome will open at the beginning of the year 2000.*
> *Eurostar will leave for Paris in ten minutes.*

Each of these examples, if spoken with emphasis on *ám* or *will*, can be made to indicate a strong colouring of intention as though contradicting assertions that these things will not happen, are impossible, or contrary to orders.

In a selection of uses of such forms referring to future time taken at random from Quiller-Couch's *The Oxford Book of English Verse 1250–1918* it is hard to find those that are not subjectively coloured. When a lover cries 'Vengeance shall fall on thy disdain' (p. 69), he is expressing or pretending to express a wish, not making a timetabling statement. When another claims, 'I loved thee once; I'll love no more' (p. 219), he is referring to an intention, or perhaps a hope for the future. Yet another feigns compulsion or obligation as far as future compositions are concerned, 'Let others sing of Knights and Paladins ... But I must sing of thee' (p 165). Real or ironic admonitions or invitations usually thought of as merely imperative ways of referring to the future are also frequent, 'O never say that I was false of heart' (p. 204), 'Rose-cheek'd Laura, come' (p. 209), 'Of Neptune's empire let us sing' (p. 209), 'Go and catch a falling star' (p. 231). It is such coloured forms that Gwendolen Harleth characteristically uses throughout *Daniel Deronda*. At first, though the form is volitional as if expressing a wish, she is able to regard them as simple predictions. The force attaching to them in the latter part of the narrative, thanks to Deronda's intervention is one of intention, no longer thought to be automatically fulfilled. In addition, there is in this section of the text a subtext of future reference involving Grandcourt, which conflicts with Gwendolen's willed intention and which she strives to suppress. The subtext speaks of wishes which fill her mind unwilled, turning her into one of those for whom 'the deed they would do starts up before them in a complete shape making a coercive type, the event they hunger for or dread rises in to vision with a seed-like growth, fading itself fast on unnumbered impressions' (p. 471).

Further possibilities of hypothetical/conditional reference to the future exist in the past forms of *shall* and *will*: *should* and *would*. For centuries English has been able to use past forms of verbs to indicate that something is contrary to fact. This was often the case in the sixteenth, seventeenth and eighteenth centuries to indicate that something might have happened but did not. When Spenser writes 'I meant *to have slain* him' (my emphasis) he means 'I meant to slay him but in fact I did not'. Or when Samuel Johnson says of Lord Chesterfield's belated offer of patronage 'Had it been early, it had been kind', he expresses succinctly the sense 'If it had been offered early it would have been kind but in fact it was not offered early, and so it was not kind'. Similarly in conditional reference to the future, use of the past forms *should* and *would* indicate not counter-factivity of Spenser's or Johnson's kind but of events somewhat removed from fact as yet: 'If I were given a free ticket I *would* go to China'; 'I *should* be grateful if you *would* send me a free ticket'. These are events that *may* happen in the future but have not yet done so.

Andrew Marvell's 'To His Coy Mistress' illustrates a pointed use of these various forms of future reference. Its opening lines express unreal expectations about the future (my emphasis):

> *Had* we but World enough, and Time,
> This coyness Lady were no crime.
> We *would sit* down and think which way
> To walk, and pass our long Loves Day.
> Thou by the Indian Ganges side
> *Shouldst* Rubies *find*: I by the Tide
> Of Humber *would complain*.

The poem is built around a contrast between this unattainable (non-factual) long stretch of time that *would have* allowed a long drawn out courtship and the contrasting brevity of actual time. The change later to a directive future captures the urgency of a wish to make the most of love's brief spell:

> Let us roll all our Strength and all
> Our sweetness, up into one Ball:
> And tear our pleasures with rough strife
> Thorough the Iron gates of Life.

A final change to the simple use of *will* is predictive or expressive of determination about the future:

> Thus though we cannot make our Sun
> Stand still, yet we *will* make him run.

(p. 399)

Different from all the subjectively coloured notions of the future are what might be seen as absolute and uncoloured predictions. These are what Lyons calls 'magical or sacramental directives': 'What is especially interesting about magical or sacramental directives ... is that (according to those who believe in their efficacy) ... [their utterance] automatically guarantees their truth' (Lyons 1978: 2.827). He cites J. L. Austin's 'I name this ship *Liberté*. But we may also include in this category of future reference such instances as biblical predictions. These, given the context of what is to Christians a divinely inspired text, are efficacious prophecies for them. On this basis the Sermon on the Mount in St Matthew's Gospel contains 'sacramental' and accurate predictions of what inevitably will come about: only the passing of time is required, as Christians believe, for these things to happen:

> Blessed are the meek: for they shall inherit the earth.
> Blessed are the merciful: for they shall obtain mercy.
> Blessed are the pure in heart: for they shall see God.
> Blessed are the peacemakers: for they shall be called the children of God.

This is the kind of magic-future reference that Mordecai typically makes, using *will* and *shall* in an evidently uncoloured way. He is able to persuade Deronda to his view of the future and so to bring about conflict with Gwendolen's. Her belief in her power to predict is shown to be erroneous but that raises questions about Deronda's own power too, as will be shown. The original perspective of the text at Leubrunn's casino is narrowly and intensely personal, based on Gwendolen's prospective future, both immediate and long-term.

Although the title leads the reader to expect a focus on the man, Daniel Deronda, he is already displaced from that position at the opening by a nameless woman:

> Was she beautiful or not beautiful? and what was the secret of form or expression which gave a dynamic quality to her glance? Was the good or the evil genius dominant in these beams? Probably the evil; or else why was the effect that of unrest rather than of undisturbed charm? (p. 7)

The passage raises questions other than those it contains: what is the woman and who is the man? Is the watcher over-fanciful in reading moral ambivalence into her appearance since she is evoked merely as the creation of his gaze? But soon the reactions of other observers confirm his sense of an unstable identity. One onlooker observes that she 'got herself up as a sort of serpent now, all green and silver', she is a 'Lamia-beauty', 'a serpent woman' (p. 8) like the central figure in Keats's poem 'Lamia' who seeks to destroy her lovers. Another spectator finds in her only a very pretty girl with 'a warm paleness' of complexion and thinks that 'there never was a prettier mouth' (p. 8). The enigma she poses is one formulated by Belsey in terms of the insistent question 'What is Gwendolen Harleth?' which replaces the 'Who is Daniel Deronda?' that the title suggests (Widdowson 1982: 131). The difficulty of fixing her identity is reiterated by the narrator at the archery meeting when she asserts that a portrait of her by a painter like Reynolds could not have represented the truth of change but merely given 'stability to one beautiful moment' (p. 102). From the start Gwendolen is oriented towards the future, as her preoccupation with gambling indicates. Before they are even named, the first lines of the text place her and Deronda in intimate juxtaposition. And the opening question 'Was she beautiful or not beautiful?' crystallizes his interest as physical attraction. The effect is enhanced by his supposedly chivalrous repurchase of her pawned necklace and its supposedly anonymous return to her like the lover's trinket she half treats it as later. Their relationship is given a particular and romantic emphasis suggesting future possibilities which caused frustration for contemporary critics. It is sustained, even prolonged, by Grandcourt's disapproval of it once he marries her. Her husband's suspicious surveillance lends a tension to their subsequent meetings. When Deronda meets her as Grandcourt's fiancée at his uncle's request, he looks forward to the projected visit with 'less disinclination' once he knows that she will be there because 'in the movement which had led him to redeem Gwendolen's necklace for her, and which was at work in him still, there was something beyond his habitual compassionate fervour – something due to the fascination of her womanhood' (p. 298). Although he has already met Mirah, Gwendolen seems more decidedly attractive than before. Once she is a married woman and forbidden fruit, he is aware of her possessing more of 'that tender appealing charm which we call womanly' (p. 378). Merely because she is beautiful and her back is turned to him he longs to go and speak to her. With Grandcourt watching even when his back is turned, their snatched moments take on a particular romantic urgency. Their brevity and danger lend them the kind of emphasis given elsewhere in the text to the allusions to contemporary national uprisings. Deronda finds himself 'acutely touched by the brief incidents and words which made the history of his intercourse with Gwendolen' (p. 384). And for her every meeting is a perceived crisis.

Paradoxically, the past is usually crucial for Eliot to the questions of identity raised here. Origins are equated with the past, especially the childhood past. But here emphasis is placed on Gwendolen's rootlessness. The sequence of the narrative disturbs strict chronological order to place her origins at the roulette table, in a foreign city, surrounded by strangers. Already fatherless, as is revealed later, she is effectively orphaned by the text. What more rootless than a gambler in transit? The fact is given added force by the narrator when Gwendolen is summoned to Offendene from Leubrunn and its casino by financial disaster:

> Pity that Offendene was not the home of Miss Harleth's childhood or endeared to her by family memories! A human life, I think, should be well-rooted in some spot of a native land, where it may get the love of tender kinship for the face of the earth, for the labours men go forth to, for the sounds and accents that haunt it, for whatever will give that early home a familiar unmistakeable difference amidst the widening of knowledge. (p. 18)

As the narrator insists, 'this blessed persistence in which affection can take root had been wanting in Gwendolen's life' (p. 22). Even her surname, Harleth, isolates her from her twice-married mother Mrs Davilow and her younger Davilow half-sisters (to whom she is at worst unkind, at best indifferent). The whole casino episode represents Gwendolen as a figure for a rootless and degenerate society, cut off from her past and focusing on a future seen solely in terms of self-interest. In Eliot's terms she and her society are badly in need of redemption.

Surprisingly, given the personal and romantic focus of the first scenes, Deronda at this point disappears from Gwendolen's sight and the reader's. In chapters three to twenty, Gwendolen's immediate past is recapitulated: her experience at Offendene with Grandcourt, her meeting with his mistress Lydia Glasher, and her consequent flight to Leubrunn to avoid a formal proposal. Since these interpolated scenes are the only major interruption to strict chronological order in the narrative, this small segment of Gwendolen's life is made subordinate to the startling opening in the casino. It is the present and, as it soon appears, the future that are the subject here. The question 'What is Gwendolen Harleth?' has a corollary: and what will become of her? Her view of her life is limited to the small circle around her lit by the candle of her egotism, the 'narrow theatre which life offers to a girl of twenty, who cannot conceive herself as anything else than a lady' (p. 56). She believes the future to be determined by her wishes and needs: they seem to her to be prophetic of what will happen. This view is for her confirmed by a belief that she is fortune's favourite, destined for a life of 'luxurious ease' (p. 12). At the roulette table she imagines a future in which she will be followed by 'a *cortège* who would worship her as a goddess of luck and watch her play as a directing augury. Such things had been known of male gamblers; why should not a woman have a like supremacy?' (p. 6). As an 'empress of luck' she is similarly fearless of her fate at the hunt. She can ride recklessly if she pleases because she confidently believes that 'no ill-luck would happen to her' (p. 64). She expects to win the archery contest 'believing in her own good fortune even more than in her skill' (p. 104).

Her wishes and hopes appear to her as simple uncoloured predictions of the future. Her life *must* necessarily turn out as it has done in the past:

> Always she was the princess in exile, who in time of famine was to have her breakfast-roll made of the finest-bolted flour from the seven thin ears of wheat, and in a general decampment *was to have* her silver fork kept out of the baggage. (p. 35)

In an only half-joking magic prediction, she speaks of her effect upon the still-unknown Grandcourt:

> My arrow *will* pierce him before he has time for thought. He *will* declare himself my slave – I *shall* send him round the world to bring me back the wedding-ring of a happy woman … he *will* come back Lord Grandcourt – but without the ring – and fall at my feet – I *shall* laugh at him. (p. 85)

She feels able, in fact, 'to manage her own destiny' (p. 35).

This narrow solipsistic universe is seen by many critics as an awkward contrast to the ever-widening vision of Deronda, driven by Mordecai. Unlike Gwendolen, Deronda feels himself 'in no sense free' (p. 148). This is because his uncertainty as to his parentage focuses his attention on the mystery of his past. Gwendolen is content to discard hers, but he longs to link his present to the past. One of his favourite protests is against the 'severance of past and present history' (p. 190). Ultimately he wishes to link the past to the future to let it determine his life in the way Eliot so strongly approves of. His education is dogged by a lack of interest in detail and a desire to know 'the principles which form the vital connections of knowledge' (p. 164). His focus is on things and people outside himself. This broad intellectual vision is linked, as Eliot linked it in *Middlemarch*, with distant physical prospects, such as the view that Mordecai admires while awaiting his spiritual heir at sunset over the river Thames. At first Deronda's longings are unspecific but he does know that he seeks a future choice of destinations. Gwendolen is looking only for the wealth that will transport her to the luxurious ease that she takes to be her destination/destiny.

Her domestic and personal focus does not accommodate national or international events which are invisible to her. But broader views constitute the frame into which Gwendolen's story is unobtrusively but firmly set. The reader is made significantly aware of contemporary events in which struggles appear involving whole nations attempting to determine *their* future. Gwendolen, however, is unaware of this 'fermenting political and social leaven which was making a difference in the history of the world' (p. 718). This persists in spite of the developments which cause her family's bankruptcy. Signs of this ferment are significantly introduced by the narrator at that point in the text shortly after she first goes to live at Offendene and there is news of Grandcourt's impending arrival at Diplow:

> Eight months after the arrival of the family at Offendene, that is to say in the end of the following June, a rumour was spread in the neighbourhood which to many persons was matter of exciting interest. It had no reference to the results of the American war, but it was one which touched all classes within a certain circuit round Wancester. (p. 81)

The specific time mentioned indicates that this was June 1865 when the American Civil War between Northern and Southern states had ended. The significance of this is rendered invisible to Gwendolen and her society by the fact that 'the corn factors, the brewers, the horse dealers and sadlers … the blacksmith … the farmers' will make more profits from Grandcourt and his entourage. For 'their betters' there will be similar distractions involving business as well as pleasure figured in 'a floating indeterminate vision of marriage in several well-bred imaginations' (p. 81). The brevity of the reference to the war serves to enact the relative unimportance this huge event has for Gwendolen and those around her, but not to diminish its force in the text.

The narrative in this early domestic and personal section is punctuated by similar references indicating a world in tumult ignored by the protagonists as they focus on their personal futures. So, after the chapter in which Gwendolen's first meeting with Grandcourt is observed in the minute detail of close-up, the perspective suddenly changes at the conclusion:

> Could there be a slenderer, more insignificant thread in human history than this consciousness of a girl, busy with her small inferences of the way in which she could make her life pleasant? – in a time, too, when ideas were with fresh vigour making armies of themselves, and the universal kinship was declaring itself fiercely: when women on the other side of the world would not mourn for their husbands and sons who died bravely in a common cause, and men stinted of bread on the other side of the world heard of that willing loss and were patient. (p. 109)

This is an allusion to the way in which English cotton-manufacturers accepted the hardship caused them by the American Civil War because of their sympathy with the anti-slavery Northern States. It was the Northern blockade preventing the Southern States from exporting cotton in 1861 which damaged the Lancashire cotton mills by depriving them of raw materials.

Gwendolen imagines herself in a timeless world of princesses in exile, but the narrator relentlessly marks the passing of specific national upheavals that go by unnoticed. In this same section of the narrative where Gwendolen, expecting compliments on her singing from Klesmer, receives none, the reader is again addressed: 'Was there ever so unexpected an assertion of superiority? at least before the late Teutonic conquests?' (p. 42). The reader at least does not remain unaware of the contemporaneous conquest of Austria by Bismarck, the German Chancellor, in 1866. Gwendolen's empire is the neighbourhood of Offendene but always present to the narrator's consciousness is the Empire, its nature and its insurrections. Klesmer, a Jewish idealist in such matters, does not take kindly to the 'expectant peer' Mr Bult's views on Empire and economic imperialism generally. Bult has 'strong opinions concerning the districts of the Niger, was much at home also in the Brazils, spoke with decision of affairs in the South Seas' (p. 223). His pompous imperialism leads Klesmer to launch an attack on 'the lack of idealism in English politics' (p. 223), a reference linking him to Deronda's later idealistic attitudes. Bult's reaction is to assume that Klesmer is 'a Panslavist', i.e. one who supports the Slav struggle for independence which eventually led (in 1875) to a Bosnian revolt against the Turks which spread to include Bulgaria, Serbia and Montenegro. All these allusions relate to struggles for a national or racial freedom and, though unelaborated, would have powerful meaning for contemporary readers. The initial scene in the casino, where Gwendolen and Deronda do silent battle with their exchanges of gaze, is echoed ironically by vast struggles from which the future will emerge on the larger scene.

The reason for these struggles is oppression of an economic as well as a political kind which in microcosm is mirrored by the fact that Gwendolen finds herself penniless after the loss of her family fortunes. She still imagines she can extend her narrow theatre to take in a wider audience for a lucrative reward. Convinced of this, she consults the musician Klesmer:

> I *must* get my own bread ... The only way I can think of – and I *should like* it better than anything – is to be an actress – to go on the stage. But of course I should like to take a high position. (p. 234)

Here the phrasing *should like* is not so much a reference to an open possibility as the use of the past form of *shall* to indicate politeness (compare, for example, 'And what was the name?' for 'What is your name?'). All she requires from Klesmer is practical advice. When he points out her inadequacies she is for once deprived of a visionary future of luxury and adulation: she 'was too much oppressed by what was near to her, in both the past and the future, for her to project her anticipations very far off' (p. 253).

So she sees herself as the oppressed, not the oppressor that she is to those around her. When Grandcourt proposes – in effect for the second time – she is overcome 'by the suffused sense that here in this man's homage to her lay the rescue from helpless subjection to an oppressive lot' (p. 279). She perceives her acceptance of him as entailing so little that her vision is now 'filled by her sense of a miraculous escape from a role as the Momperts' governess'. She feels confidently able to prophecy their future in new magic terms: 'You *are not* going to Sawyer's Cottage, I *am not* going to be inspected by Mrs Mompert, and everything *is to be* as I like' (p. 282). But again she is mistaken about her ability to control the future. Her predictions are not matched by a context which would lend them efficacy. Control of her life passes to Grandcourt and unwittingly she becomes the oppressed not the oppressor.

The significance of this psychological study of a woman who is the apotheosis of Lady Audley in this kind of society is the focus of recent critical discussion. For some it makes the Jewish section involving Mordecai and Deronda an irrelevant appendage; for others it is represented as a contrast to the wider horizons and altruistically selfless approach to national life of the two men. Such a reading sees Gwendolen's 'psychological imperialism' as a metaphor for her class and for her culture with 'the domestic and sexual politics of Gwendolen's private life being linked to the imperialist policies of colonialization and exploitation' (Linehan 1992: 324). Ironically, she sees herself as having an imperialist control over the future in the satisfaction of her wishes for the hottest coffee and crispest toast, and obtaining an expensive horse from her uncle. But after her marriage to Grandcourt it becomes clear that hers was an imagined imperialism. She has oppressively selfish instincts but no power beyond the domestic. As Linehan notes, the language of power and empire is transferred to her husband who has all the power that money, an aristocratic standing and a white skin can buy. In accepting him she is not taking control over him: she believes that she is 'getting a sort of empire over her own life' and future (p. 271). But he has the money and the power to determine their future in a way she fails to see.

Gwendolen, with the future, as she believes, hers to predict, expects to have 'indefinite power' (p. 288) over Grandcourt, once married to him. This mistress–servant role is the only one she can conceive of. The marriage certainly figures a power relationship and nothing else; but it is that of master and slave, not mistress and servant. Grandcourt is about to teach her about the meaning of imperial power for those on whom it is imposed. Its extent is measured by his capacity to exact satisfaction by imposing humiliation and suffering. This is the basis of his treatment for every creature he encounters. He seems to require these extreme reactions in others in order to stir his lizard-like and inert personality to feelings of pleasure. Dogs, horses, servants and women are all subject to his regime of torment. He caresses one dog solely in order to drive another to 'amusing anguish', until his pleasure at the anguish gives way to irritation. Then, since a gentleman requires someone else to kick his dogs for him, he orders Lush to 'Turn out that brute' (p. 111). Lush too has a clear understanding that he must be 'kickable' (p. 114). Like Gwendolen, his reward is to be given material luxury.

Grandcourt wishes to marry Gwendolen largely because she resists him in a spirited way. He sees her in the same light as a spirited horse whom he can take pleasure in breaking. He feels later that she has 'been brought to accept him in spite of everything – brought to kneel down like a horse under training for the arena' (p. 293). She has come to fear this early in the marriage and for once realistically predicts: 'he delights in making the dogs and horses quail: that is half his pleasure in calling them his ... It *will come to be* so with me and I *shall quail*' (p. 398). The implications of this for their sexual relationship are tacit but powerful. He himself thinks that he holds his wife 'with bit and bridle' (p. 633). He demonstrates this by making her accompany him on the fatal yachting trip as they both recognize, 'to feel more securely that she was his to do as he liked with, and to make her feel it also' (p. 622).

For Grandcourt dogs, horses, servants and women can all, in terms of rights, be grouped with the slave, 'the Jamaican negro' of whom he says to Deronda that he is 'a beastly sort of baptist Caliban' (p. 303). This refers to the rebellious George William Gordon, son of a white woman and a black slave. He was executed in 1865 by the notoriously ruthless Governor Eyre who was responsible for the crushing of the rebellion in Jamaica. Later the equation between Grandcourt and Eyre is made specific. He forbids Gwendolen to visit Mirah saying, 'What do *you* know about the world? You have married *me*, and must be guided by my opinion' (p. 552; original emphasis). The narrator comments

> He knew the force of his own words. If this white-handed man with the perpendicular profile had been sent to govern a difficult colony, he might have won reputation among his contemporaries. He had certainly ability, would have understood that it was safer to exterminate than to cajole superseded proprietors, and would not have flinched from making things safe in that way. (p. 552)

This is the point at which the central concerns of the text – gender, class and race – manifestly connect with each other. Gwendolen's belief in her imperial power to control what is to happen had enabled her to take her wishes for the future as uncoloured and valid predictions. She mistook them for magic futures in which 'Everything is *to be* as I like' (p. 282). With the transfer not merely of the language of imperial power from his wife to Grandcourt but the reality of it as well, their marriage is seen to focus much large larger issues. These are those ironically marginalized but relentlessly memorialized by the text. Clearly the union is seen to symbolize through the power relations of gender, those of class and race. The submissive posture of a prospective husband is shown to be a polite and temporary fiction. Grandcourt's treatment of his dogs, horses, servants and wife is coolly represented as the natural behaviour of an upper-class imperialist. His aristocratic domination over the farmers, blacksmiths and tradesmen dependent on his patronage to an extent that blots out news of war elsewhere, has the same rationale as the husband's over his wife and the white man's over the black. Grandcourt's expert oppression of Gwendolen, conducted without violence, makes her domestic and sexual life a powerful figure for what Linehan calls the 'actual imperialist policies of colonization and exploitation' (Linehan 1992: 324).

Significantly, it is hard to see the Jewish race similarly figured by this union between Grandcourt and Gwendolen. In the anti-semitic orthodoxy of the time, some Jewish reviewers were, as Martin points out, eager to praise what they saw as Eliot's sympathy with and understanding of Judaism. One asserts in the *Jewish Chronicle* that the work is 'of the deepest interest to Jewish readers' (Martin 1988: 92). Another, defending Deronda's acceptance of Judaism asks

before he meets with Mordecai what noble work in life has this young
and cultured Englishman? … This age of unfaith gives no outlet for
his deep, spiritual yearnings … Yet there comes to this ardent soul an
angel of the Lord (albeit in the shape of a poor Jew watch-mender).
(Martin 1988: 96).

In line with this, some more recent critics have argued precisely as
does Hirsch that 'Her contemporary readers had failed to see the connections she had forged between the condition of Jews in Britain and
the condition of women in British society at a specific moment in history. She sees both groups as being 'exiles, homeless and powerless'
(Hirsch 1994: 45). This is to ignore the economic facts so crucial to
this narrative. Gwendolen is open to her oppressive marriage, in spite
of her beauty and spirit, because she is fatherless, penniless and her
family is ruined. On the other hand Deronda, though Jewish, is effort-
lessly wealthy by inheritance. He is economically free to make choices
even of the options that Sir Hugo regards as 'eccentricities'. In addition
the other upper-class Jewish figure, Klesmer, is rich enough to mix
with the upper class and gifted with a musical talent which gives him
the grand status of 'genius'. He carries off the richest woman in the
novel despite parental disapproval.

The expectation here is that the position of Jews in society will also
be figured by this union of oppressor and victim. As Cheyette (1993)
points out, the representation of 'the Jews' is slippery, offering conflicting accounts. The satire on English upper-class anti-Semitism is
plain. Sir Hugo tries to turn Deronda, despite his Jewish origins, into
an English gentleman, free from any but acceptable eccentricities. His
wife, on hearing that Mirah is Jewish, helpfully observes that there is
a Society for the Conversion of the Jews and that it is to be hoped
that the girl will embrace Christianity. Deronda himself is seen to share
this distaste for Jewishness and it is unclear whether he alone, or the
narrator with him, sees Mrs Cohen in this light. The narrative describes her at this point with 'her look of having made her toilet with
little water, and by twilight … and of having presumably slept in her
long earrings' (Cheyette 1993: 48). This picture signifies what Cheyette
calls 'the Jews' as 'a degenerate contemporary race', alongside the alternative figure that Mordecai represents which is 'quasi-biblical, spiritual community rooted in the past' (p. 48). Her husband also is coarse

and ugly, with an added oily persuasiveness and evident greed for money, 'no shadow of a Suffering Race distinguished his vulgarity of soul ...' (p. 362). Even the child Jacob bartering for a pocket knife is a miniature usurer: 'His small voice was hoarse in its glibness, as if it belonged to an aged commercial soul, fatigued with bargaining through many generations' (p. 360). Some critics have read all this as a satirical critique of anti-Semitism; but as Heller points out,

> The evident purpose of these unattractive Jews is to balance, and therefore give credibility to, the more ideal Jews. What is distressing about them, however, is that their unattractiveness is automatically presented as having a peculiarly Jewish flavour, as conforming, in short, to pre-established negative stereotypes. (Heller and Cohen 1990: 86)

The Jewish race in fact is not presented as victimized, whether it is represented by the alternatives of Deronda, Mordecai, Klesmer or the Cohens. There is no equation offered between the relationship of Gwendolen to Grandcourt and that between the Jewish and English communities. In this way the central figure of the oppressive marriage fails to connect the Jewish story with everything else in the text.

Grandcourt's powerful position in the economic system of exchange that constitutes society means that his wishes and commands are truly valid predictions requiring only the passing of time to bring about their fulfilment. His future reference is magical: its efficacy is ensured by his wealth and position. He can therefore with reason use the uncoloured verb forms or commands with absolute confidence in their predictive power. Gwendolen may repeat to herself up to the moment of her acceptance, that she will not marry him, but from the first he tells Lush 'I *am going to* marry her' (p. 113). And of course he is proved right, despite her mother's wretched experience of marriage, and her knowledge of Lydia Glasher and her illegitimate children. He can buy her as a man buys horses, dogs, servants and slaves. Because of this fact, Gwendolen's belief that she can confidently gamble and trust to her luck is shown as a pitiful mistake. On her wedding day she still pictures herself 'standing at the game of life with many eyes upon her, daring everything to win much' (pp. 326–7). She soon learns the truth – that marriage is not a gamble but a bargain, a piece of trading in which there is both loss and gain:

Grandcourt might have pleaded that he was perfectly justified in taking care that his wife should fulfill the obligations she had accepted. Her marriage was a contract where all the ostensible advantages were on her side, and it was only one of those advantages that her husband should use his power to hinder her from any injurious self-committal or unsuitable behaviour. He knew quite well that she had not married him … out of love to him personally; he had won her by the rank and luxuries he had to give her and these she had got: he had fulfilled his side of the contract. (p. 623)

This accurate account of the role of women in the society of the novel sees them as what Gallagher calls 'items of exchange, a form of currency and a type of commodity' (p. 40). It is the latter fact that Gwendolen has failed to understand. She has seen herself as a lucky seller without realizing that in selling herself she becomes a commodity just as much as a slave purchased in the market. All the middle-class women in *Daniel Deronda* with one exception, Catherine Arrowpoint, are commodities: she, because she understands trading, rejects marriage with an impoverished peer. Lydia Glasher, Grandcourt's mistress who erupts into Gwendolen's life like 'some ghastly vision' in a dream, saying with all the authority of an omnetemporal present tense 'I am a woman's life' (p. 137), is willingly bought by his wealth and diamonds. Deronda's mother, the famous singer Al Charisi (a.k.a. Princess Halm Eberstein), tells how she escaped from her father's possession to avoid being handed to another man in an arranged marriage. She sold herself to a man she did not love in order to pursue her career. Mirah's father tries to act as her pimp until she escapes by flight. She is taken up randomly like flotsam by Deronda on the riverbank and transferred in marriage to Deronda by her dying brother.

In this she appears to be acting as a surrogate for Mordecai whose relationship with Deronda involves the feminine characteristics of the latter. These have been indicated from boyhood onwards in his shame at the thought of illegitimacy and his unwillingness to fight at school where 'unlike the great Clive' (and Grandcourt) he 'would rather be the calf than the butcher' (p. 162). His mind too shows 'the same blending of child's ignorance with surprising knowledge which is oftener seen in bright girls' (p. 151). With Sir Hugo he is 'moved by an affectionateness such as we are apt to call feminine, disposing him to yield in ordinary details' (p. 295). His reactions to his mother's decision to part from him shows 'that all the woman lacking in her was present in him' (p. 615). Above all he is feminine in his compassion and altruistic concern for others which were the 'essential' virtues for the ideal woman of the time. As Leslie Stephen noted in 1881, Deronda is to be included in those men who in Eliot's work are 'simply women in disguise' (Carroll 1971: 474).

This feminising of Deronda facilitates the representation of the relationship with Mordecai as that of destined lovers. Mordecai's vision is the magic future in which he will meet the 'awaited friend', 'his executive self'. He feels 'a mature spiritual need akin to the boy's and girl's picturing of the future beloved' (p. 442) for whom he hungers with 'a strong love' (p. 443). By a sleight of hand on the part of the narrator, Mordecai's prophecy of a strong, young, beautiful lover is apparently fulfilled. In the semi-religious and overtly symbolic setting of sunset on the Thames as Deronda gazes out at a wide vista, he sees the future beloved being rowed towards him: 'the nearing figure lifted up its face towards him – the face of his visions – and then immediately, with white uplifted hand, beckoned again and again' (p. 459). In this Tennysonian incident the gender of the figure is concealed by the pronoun, while the white hand suggests a woman. This event prefaces a scene where the two men, alone in a gas-lit bookshop, regard each other 'with as intense a consciousness as if they had been two undeclared lovers' (p. 462). Their love is as yet undeclared because at this point Deronda does not know that he is a Jew who can become the other's 'second self'. Their intense relationship, so often insisted on, makes Mirah merely a link in the chain of events that leads Deronda to Mordecai.

It is here that a critic like Cheyette (1993) would locate the overt significance of 'the Jews' in *Daniel Deronda*: in the redemption of an Englishness which is losing its proper sense of nationhood and becoming as cosmopolitan, hybrid and rootless as the gamblers at Leubronn. As he sees it, by contrast with Matthew Arnold's hope in *Culture and Anarchy* (1869), for 'universalist Hellenized Jews as a *tabula rasa* for the inscription of the ideal of 'culture' is self-consciously reversed in *Daniel Deronda*' (Cheyette 1993: 43). In this version Judaism is the transcendent form of burning nationalism which can transform a degenerate English culture. It is the relationship of Deronda to Mordecai (who is

absent from the earlier section of the narrative) that figures the transformation. Mordecai's appropriation of Daniel awkwardly displaces the
Gwendolen–Deronda pairing so strongly emphasized in earlier chapters.

By the time of the deadly sailing trip Gwendolen at last has clearly
recognized her commodity status:

> she felt that she had sold herself, and had been paid the strict price –
> nay, paid more than she had dared to ask in the handsome mainte-
> nance of her mother: the husband to whom she had sold her truth-
> fulness and sense of justice so that he held them throttled into si-
> lence, collared and dragged behind him to witness what he could
> without remonstrance'. (p. 623)

She has assumed that she only paid with her physical self but discovers that the price was more Faustian. Her feelings echo those of the
runaway slave Frederick Douglass, who wrote in 1845 of one of his
masters

> If at any one time of my life more than another I was made to drink
> the bitterest dregs of slavery that time was during the first six months
> of my stay with Mr. Covey, … I was somewhat unmanageable when
> I first went there, but a few months of this discipline tamed me.
> Mr. Covey succeeded in breaking me. I was broken in body, soul,
> and spirit. My natural elasticity was crushed, my intellect languished,
> … the dark light of slavery closed in upon me. (Baker 1986: 105)

When Gwendolen discovers her true position, she consciously seeks
a new future by turning again to Deronda for help. He teaches her that
gambling does not work; and therefore she expects him to provide another way of managing her life. In place of her lost belief that her wishes
are predictions, he can only offer a didactic aphorism endowed with all
the authority of the (omnetemporal, true-at-all-times) present tense:

> There are enough inevitable turns of fortune which force us to see
> that our gain is another's loss – that is one of the ugly aspects of life.
> One would like to reduce it as much as one could, not get amuse-
> ment out of exaggerating it. (p. 309)

Though as yet she does not understand it, 'our gain is another's loss'
becomes her mantra and that of the text, taking in past, present and

future. Acceptance of the idea would do more than put a stop to gambling: it would throw a spanner into the works of a capitalist society at large. Yet, paradoxically it is accepted by the narrator as offering an illuminating perspective on gender, class and race. All these depend on systems of exchange involving a 'superior' who gains and to whom the losses of his inferiors (slaves, labourers, women) are irrelevant. Grandcourt, living on his inherited wealth, is able to enjoy 'the piquancy of despotism'. His contempt for blacks and slaves is matched by his belief that 'all commercial men, and all voters liable to use the wrong kind of soap' are 'brutes'. As such they do not merit trade unions or household suffrage (p. 543).

Gwendolen struggles to unfold Deronda's axiom. She sees it as a key to a projected future in which – unusually for her – *perhaps* she may be free from her claustrophobic sense of degradation. This is reminiscent of the escaped slave – Frederick Douglass's statement that his master Covey (who like Grandcourt resembles 'the snake' which is his nickname) 'had the faculty of making us feel that he was ever present with us' (Baker, 1986:103). Thus Deronda has already acted as a 'priest', and he now acts as Christian missionaries were supposed to do by giving Gwendolen a sense of sin which sabotages her psychic economy. Terms that she thought could be grasped like coins slip from her. The straightforward business of wagering a stake and winning a profit dissolves before her eyes. Even simple arithmetic no longer holds: marriage is all a 'part of that new gambling in which the losing was not simply a *minus* but a terrible *plus* that had never entered her reckoning' (p. 556; original emphasis). Though in this context the 'terrible *plus*' is the reappearance of the hated Lush, there is more implied than this. It is never referred to but throughout the marriage the breaking of Gwendolen, the insistence by Grandcourt on her proximity on the yacht, her dread of becoming pregnant, all imply the kind of sexual relationship that might be expected with a man as coldly sadistic as her husband.

Ironically it is from Grandcourt not from Deronda that she learns about gain and loss. He teaches her a new pragmatism. She no longer assumes that her desires are straightforward predictions that are naturally bound to be fulfilled. She even begins not to feel sure what desire is. She has not questioned whether her wishes are under her control. Now this changes: 'Side by side with the dread of her husband had grown the self-dread which urged her to flee from the pursuing images wrought by her pent-up impulse' (p. 627). In one way she begins to think of the future as a calculation rather than a gamble. In trying to find an escape from the prison of her marriage, she shows an unfamiliar pragmatism. When she tells herself 'I *will* insist on being separated from him' (p. 560), she recognizes this as a forlorn hope or wish, not a certain prediction. She can no longer assume that this wish is a predictive statement because the real consequences of her actions are now something she takes into account. If she leaves her husband, her mother '*would be* made destitute'. 'What *could* she say to justify her flight?' 'What future lay before her gone back to her mother?' The move into a conditional future, a grasp of 'what if ...' revealed in these thoughts represents a new stage in her understanding of how things come about. Her own phrase 'I *will* insist on separation' is revealed to her as 'an easy combination of words; but considered as an action to be executed against Grandcourt, it would be about as practical as to give him a pliant disposition' (p. 561). The only clear prediction she can make is that there is 'no effort at freedom that would not bring fresh and worse humiliation' (p. 515).

Alongside this clear-eyed look at what will come about, develop unwilled impulses which to Gwendolen's horror seem out of her control. Her strangling of her sister's canary now seems to have been a foreshadowing of her preoccupation with images of death by strangulation or garroting, a familiar form of assault at the time on the nighttime streets of London. Sometimes it is she who feels threatened by 'throttling' at the white hands of Grandcourt when he is forcing her to wear the diamonds taken from his mistress. She feels that he has 'throttled into silence' her truthfulness and sense of justice' (p. 623). Another equation offers itself to her unasked: he has throttled her into a state of emotional death, and she will throttle him. This is conveyed not in the utterance of wishes but in dream-like daytime images which beset her:

> The thought that his dying was the only possible deliverance for her was one with the thought that deliverance would never come ... the thought of his dying would not subsist. It turned as with a dream-change into the terror that she would die with his throttling fingers on her neck avenging that thought. (p. 564)

The images do at last identify themselves to her as strong wishes. When she is trapped alone in a small boat with her husband

> She was not afraid of any outward dangers – she was afraid of her own wishes, which were taking shapes possible and impossible, like a cloud of demon-faces. She was afraid of her own hatred, which under the cold iron touch that had compelled her to-day had gathered a fierce intensity. (p. 635)

She has become a divided self with a desire to break out of her entrapment by committing murder, battling with a nascent conscience. Like Frederick Douglass she is impelled to the kind of insurrection that parallels the Indian Mutiny and the Jamaican uprising. His sense of tormenting confinement is echoed by hers. As the slave Douglass reads, he discovers how he came to be a slave stolen from Africa:

> I have often wished myself a beast. I preferred the condition of the meanest reptile to my own. Any thing, no matter what, to get rid of thinking! It was this everlasting thinking of my condition that tormented me. There was no getting rid of it. It was pressed upon me by every object within sight or hearing, animal or inanimate. (Baker 1986: 84)

Gwendolen's murderous impulse persists long enough to stay her hand when Grandcourt falls into the water and drowns. The commercial transaction which was her marriage turns into a nightmarish trade-off, as she repays her husband with death by drowning in return for his throttling of her sense of self. In doing this she has come to understand that her murderous impulses were truly predictions, as were the images of dead faces that she saw or imagined. This reveals to her a future not controllable by conscious wishes. For Eliot marriage and murder seem to be intimately related. Her earlier victim of marital suffocation, Dorothea Brooke in *Middlemarch* (1871–72), speaks in terms of such an equation (made in the present tense) to Rosamund Vincy as though telling of an omnetemporal truth: 'Marriage is so unlike anything else. There is something awful even in the nearness it brings'. Preference for a man other than the husband 'murders our marriage – and then the marriage stays with us like a murder' (chapter 81). Certainly this describes Gwendolen's experience after Grandcourt's death when she cannot shake off her guilt: 'I did kill him in my thoughts' (p. 647).

It is her preference for Deronda which leads her to turn to him as her priest/lover, although the narrator now begins to emphasize that her feelings for him are not purely romantic, an emphasis which cannot cancel the earlier representation of an electrifying bond between them. Since her absolute trust in him makes her a believer, she accepts his promise, 'I will not forsake you' (p. 643), as a simple magic prediction. She is unaware that he is on the brink of accepting Mordecai's prophecies as true and taking up a mission to found a Jewish national state far away. Deronda now knows that he is a Jew and is potentially as firm a believer in the efficacy of Mordecai's magical-future claims as a Christian is in the predictions of the Sermon on the Mount or as Gwendolen is in his promise. This is underlined by the semi-biblical language in which Mordecai has revealed his vision of the future:

> Then ideas, beloved ideas, came to me, because I was a Jew.
> They were a trust to fulfill, because I was a Jew.
> They were an inspiration, because I was a Jew. (p. 463)

To Deronda's initial agnosticism as to the truth of his references to the future, Mordecai still speaks with biblical certainty: 'You have risen within me like a thought not fully spelled … The rest *will* come' (p. 468). As to the idea that his belief in the efficacy of his claims may come to be seen as an illusion, – he calmly states his sacramental certainty that 'That hour *will* never come' (p. 469). To reinforce this, he is assumed to belong to a pre-existing category of true prophets. The narrator asserts that his is 'one of the natures where a wise estimate of consequences is fused in the fires of that passionate belief which determines the consequences it believes in' (p. 477). As he expands his vision it echoes verbally the narrator's references to contemporary nationalistic uprisings referred to as 'fermenting political and social leaven' that is making 'a difference in the history of the world' (p. 718). He, in contrast with Gwendolen, takes a wide-ranging view: he believes that 'leaven' is needed and that he knows where to find it. He even commands the future: 'What is needed is the leaven – what is needed is the seed of fire … *Let* the reason of Israel *disclose* itself in a great outward deed, and *let there be* another great migration, another choosing of Israel to be a nationality whose members may still stretch to the ends of the earth, even as the sons of England and Germany'

(p. 497). He compares the future Judaea to the Union of the American states (which had been effected after the Civil War), and is certain that its shining example 'will reach afar' (p. 498).

Once Deronda has accepted Judaism, his beliefs ensure for him the efficacy of these sacramental futures. He can discard his old beliefs and with them his promise to Gwendolen. He believes himself destined to work, in time to come, for a Jewish homeland. This is apparently the 'destination' he sought for, which Hans Meyrick, Mirah's other suitor, so aptly describes, 'But now confound you! you turn out to be in love in the right place – a Jew – and everything eligible' (p. 731). Without a struggle Deronda has reached the brink of his optimum future which the narrator translates into more grandiose terms than Hans: 'The very best of human possibilities' which is 'the blending of a complete personal love in one current with a larger duty' (p. 581). He has the easy option, in brief, of marriage to Mirah. Were it not for the blood tie between her and Mordecai and the latter's convenient death, it would surely be a bigamous one. On learning that Deronda is a Jew, Mordecai has spoken of the consummation of their union: 'It has begun already – the marriage of our souls'. Mirah is merely the seal on this 'willing marriage which melts soul into soul, and makes thought fuller as clean waters are made fuller, where the fullness is inseparable and the clearness is inseparable' (p. 698). The awkward displacement of Gwendolen by Mordecai is only potentiated when Mirah replaces her brother.

When Deronda promised not to forsake Gwendolen, he did so with the feeling that he was 'putting his name to a blank paper which might be filled up terribly' (p. 643). And now it is not for him but for Gwendolen that it is filled up in a terrible way. When he manages to tell her of his intention to marry Mirah, Gwendolen, drowning in despair, passes sentence on herself, 'I have been a cruel woman. And I am forsaken' (p. 749). As before with her, Deronda pretends to predict a magic future while really uttering an admonition: 'You have made efforts. You *will go on* making them' (p. 750). But this is really a hope not a prophecy. Still in forms expressive of certainty he seems to reinstate his promise not to forsake her 'We *shall not* be quite parted'; only to slide into a series of enfeebling qualifications 'I *will* write to you always, when I can …' (p. 750).

This is an outright betrayal of what Deronda, albeit reluctantly, offered to Gwendolen as a magic future. But in keeping with the paradoxical notion that, while she must struggle, Deronda is in the grip of a divine destiny, the narrator moves to connect his actions with the great historical forces that have been insisted on as the ever-present but unnoticed context for these individual lives:

> The thought that he might come back after going to the East, sank before the bewildering vision of these wide-stretching purposes in which she felt herself reduced to a mere speck. There comes a terrible moment to many souls when the great movements of the world, the larger destinies of mankind, which have lain aloof in newspapers and other neglected reading, enter like an earthquake into their own lives – when the slow urgency of growing generations turns into the tread of an invading arm or the dire clash of civil war, and grey fathers know nothing to seek for but the corpses of their blooming sons, and girls forget all vanity to make lint and bandages which may serve for the shattered limbs of their betrothed husbands. (p. 747–8)

But such a strained effort to relate 'everything in the book' to everything else there fails. The frantic rhetoric cannot conceal the fact that there is neither an invading army nor a civil war. Deronda's departure with Mirah to the East is only one of 'great movements of the world' for believers in the efficacy of Mordecai's prophecies about the future. Gwendolen's final words, however, dismiss the belief in a magically determined future life. She predicts only a struggle with herself, 'I *will try* to live – try to live. I *shall* think of you … It shall be the better for me –' (p. 750). It is her resolution, not any religious magic, that allows her to say to her mother 'I *am going to* live … I *shall* live. I *shall be* better.' (p. 751). This is clearly not a prediction but an intention: she has learnt the difference between commanding, wishing, intending, and predicting. Perhaps the most difficult aspects to reconcile of her story and Deronda's are her epiphany and his: she learns that the future is not controllable, and he learns that it is destined and controlled.

This, however, is only one of the ways in which the connections made by Eliot between 'everything in the book' end in contradiction. Gwendolen's resentment and Al Charisi's to the roles that society has preconstructed for them are sympathetically evoked – most strikingly in the latter's address to her son:

> You are not a woman. You must try – but you can never imagine
> what it is to have a man's force of genius in you, and yet to suffer the
> slavery of being a girl. To have a pattern cut out – 'This is the Jewish
> woman; this is what you must be; this is what you are wanted for; a
> woman's heart must be of such a size and no larger, else it must be
> pressed small, like Chinese feet, her happiness is to be made as cakes
> are, by a fixed receipt'. (p. 588)

Yet in the end Al Charisi feels impelled to submit to the demands of
'something tyrannic' and is 'forced' to tell Deronda he is a Jew (p. 588).
Gwendolen pays heavily for her egotism and having been taught to sin
is abandoned by Deronda. Even Mirah, the ideally submissive woman,
is told by Mordecai that 'women are specially formed for the love which
feels possession in renouncing ... the surpassing love, that loses self in
the object of love' (p 683). When she mildly queries the instance he
quotes from 'the later *Midrash*', he rebukes her in terms suitable for
that tainted figure, the actress: 'My sister, thou has read too many plays
... Thou judgest by the plays, and not by thy own heart, which is like
our mother's' (p. 684). Even Mirah is not quite submissive enough for
the now almost canonized figure of Mordecai. And presumably in the
projected Jewish state Mirah and her like will be ideals of womanhood,
ever meeker as they are instructed.

Similarly there is a surprising, pro-imperialist element embedded in
the account of the future Jewish state by the approving reference to the
empire-building 'sons of England and Germany' (p. 497). This is at
odds with the critique of imperial tyranny embodied in the figure of
Grandcourt. What this shows is that whereas the Jewish state is projected as the future utopia for humanity and a union of nations, it is at
the same time racially exclusive. It is somehow to be seen as non-impe-
rialistic and beneficially imperialistic, though there has been no sign of
benign empire in the text – only malign.

The final sections of the narrative constitute a partial retreat in relation to gender, race, empire. With each there is some degree of regres-
sion to a conservative or conventional view. Nor despite strenuous efforts by Eliot is the anti-Semitism evident in the representation of the
Cohens entirely suppressed. On the contrary, it is startlingly underlined: what Mordecai refers to as 'a great migration' will be, for the Jews
involved, in fact an *e*migration. At this period before the development

of full-blown Zionism, which as Meyer (1993) points out belongs to the 1890s, emigration had an unfavourable significance. This is not surprising since its ostensible use at this time was as a method of disposing of criminals, rescued prostitutes and 'redundant' single women for whom demographics showed no available husbands. Discussion in the periodicals focused on whether it was efficacious in dealing with these problems. Typical is a satirical article in the *Saturday Review* for 6 September 1862 quoted by Kranidis. It offers a generalization:

> It matters little what class it is desired to send abroad – governesses, paupers, penitents, or convicts; the principle of selection is the same. From our point of view it is natural enough … We naturally turn out the non-effectives first (Kranidis 1998: 132).

The strain of anti-Semitism in the narrative is persistent enough to lend a certain logic to the idea that the Cohens and the rest of the Jewish race would be better off emigrating to a country of their own.

Perhaps the most crucial retreat enacted by the last scenes of the text is even more fundamental to its structure than the treatment of women, Jews and empire. As was pointed out originally, the whole novel is a critique of a society where the economic power of one group over another is somehow naturalized. The key to a solution purveyed by Eliot through Deronda is for individuals not to count only gains to themselves, but the loss that gain constitutes to others. This is the aphorism that Deronda works to make real to Gwendolen until Grandcourt does the job for him. She clings to it as a lifeline in the scene where she confesses to her part in Grandcourt's death. For her, even that stems ultimately from the fact that in marrying him 'I wanted to make my gain out of another's loss' (p. 645). Deronda, taking on Mordecai's role, promises her a magic future and predicts that if she follows his advice 'You *will find* your life growing like a plant' (p. 715). Yet, as he recognizes, her 'new existence' seems to her inseparable from him. By embracing Judaism he has found the biggest gain of his life in both general and personal terms. It is impossible not to see that he does so at her expense. His gain is her loss. In presenting this as not in any way detrimental to him, Eliot endorses the ideal of entrepreneurial selfishness which puts its own gain before another's loss and destabilizes the novel's thesis.

Deixis

5

Who, when and what:
deixis in *Bleak House*

'I' is not the name of a person, nor 'here' of a place, and 'this'
is not a name. But they are connected with names.
(Wittgenstein)

VANITY FAIR has a dual narrator: who is sometimes homodiegetic –
a character in the text; and sometimes heterodiegetic and external to events. *Bleak House* (1853) divides the two functions, into a
third person heterodiegetic teller who uses the present tense and third
person, and a homodiegetic teller, Esther Summerson, who tells her
own story in the past tense and first person. Such a structure is unique
in Victorian mainstream literature. The closest parallel is James Hogg's
The Private Memoirs and Confessions of a Justified Sinner (1824), in
which the events are narrated by a third person ('the editor') and then a
first person narrator (Wringhim) separately. The latter is the sinner of
the title and each narrator uses the past tense. In both *Confessions* and
Bleak House the double narration crucially affects the significance of
the text but it does so in different ways in each. In Hogg's novel the two
narratives effectively destabilize each other. In *Bleak House* the relationship between the two accounts is more asymmetrical. Wringhim's
relevance to the story of his brother's murder is clear, the choice of
Esther out of a multitude of characters to supplement the third person's story is not. This prioritizing of her suggests a centrality, a heroine
status, with which she collaborates to the extent of offering herself as a
model of the domestic ideal. I first wish to take her story in isolation to
examine it to show its disturbingly polyvalent nature before relating it
to the wider narration. I shall do this after pointing out the potential of

the particular linguistic mechanisms of person and tense that it deploys. These mechanisms are aspects of deixis.

When Wittgenstein says that 'I' is not the name of a person, he is seeing in a linguistic feature of deixis – a significant fact. To the linguist deixis means 'the location of persons, objects, events, processes and activities being talked about or referred to, in relation to the space–time context created by the act of utterance and the participation in it, typically, of a single speaker and at least one addressee' (Lyons 1978: 2.637). What Wittgenstein is pointing out is that in such an utterance the meaning of 'I' is not fully captured by substituting a proper name or a common noun or description, such as 'Winston Smith' or 'the hero of *Nineteen Eighty-Four*'. Nor is it adequately translated as 'the speaker of this utterance'. In addition the 'I' of an utterance is malleable. My 'I' may become yours when you respond to what I say. A competitive conversation is a struggle for the possession of 'I'. The obvious significance of a first person narrative is that it orientates the world spatially and temporally around the narrator. So he or she becomes the zero point of reference for both space and time and fills the pronoun with a new identity.

The generic *Bildungsroman* often begins with an unnamed 'I' as Esther's does. This is the case with a 'true' autobiography like Ruskin's *Praeterita* (1885–89): 'I am, and my father was before me, a violent Tory of the old school; – Walter Scott's that is to say, and Homer's' (Cockshutt 1994: 5). It is the same in some 'fictional autobiographies' such as *David Copperfield* (1850): 'Whether I shall turn out to be the hero of my own life, or whether that station will be held by anybody else, the pages must show' (Blount 1996: 49). The 'I's of such accounts, whether fictional or theoretically non-fictional, engage in the same activity: looking back on a series of events and experiences. Both construct a coherent and plausible story by making connections between them and so literally 'making' sense out of them. Events will be selected for their supposed significance so that making sense in such texts is always a creative process. Selection is necessary because, as Nancy K. Miller puts it, 'in life, unlike art, anything can happen: hence the constraints of likeliness do not apply' (Miller 1988: 25). As Shuttleworth points out, in the nineteenth century new theories of subjectivity developed: 'Selfhood no longer resided in the open texture of social act and exchange, but within a new interior space, hidden from view, inaccessible even to the subject's own consciousness' (Shuttleworth 1996: 9). It is within this framework that Dickens, like Charlotte Brontë, writes his fictional autobiographies.

Openings such as those of *Praeterita* and *David Copperfield* raise the question 'Who is this 'I' that is making himself the centre of everything by relating time and space to his perspectives and by claiming to be their zero point of reference?' This is the very question to which the first-person narrative constructs a reply. By telling 'his' or 'her' story the narrator learns to control the past and so creates an identity. The underlying assumption of telling oneself such a story is that the very memory of linked past sequences of experiences is proof of the continuous and continued identity of a single self. There is no similarly urgent need for this with a third-person narrator who is external to events in the text. His or her identity is in place and often screened by anonymity. The implication of the opening of this kind of narrative is that it has some other related, perhaps larger or loftier, aim in view than the purely personal. This expansive tone is evident in the detachment of the opening lines of E. M. Forster's *A Passage to India* (1922–24): 'Except for the Marabar Caves – and they are twenty miles off – the city of Chandrapore presents nothing extraordinary' (Stallybrass 1985: chapter 1). The question implied here is not 'who is this person?' but 'what is extraordinary about these particular caves?'

What then does it involve if a narrating 'I' is the zero point of reference for time? Time is of two kinds: the kind on a clock face and the kind we fabricate when we speak or write in the first person. This means that my egocentric past was once some other speaker's future; my future will be some other speaker's past, as my 'here' is some other person's 'there'. In the world of discourse peculiar to a given text such individual constructions and reconstructions are possible. As a speaking 'I', telling the story of my life and dealing with what has happened so far, I claim a stretch of time from the past and shape it into 'my' story. For such a narrative the tense used in English is the time-bound past that Esther uses. This does not mean that the present tense which is used by the third person narrator in *Bleak House* is similarly bound to the present time. It may be used as a commentary on a football match or coronation contemporaneous with the utterance. But commentary time-bound to the present is not its only use. It may even refer to the future: 'I go on holiday tomorrow'. Each of these three uses of the present tense is time-bound but there are others. The opening of W. H. Auden's 'Roman Wall Blues' sounds like commentary alluding to an immediate experience:

> Over the heather the wet wind blows,
> I've lice in my tunic and a cold in my nose,
> The rain comes pattering out of the sky,
> I'm a Wall soldier, I don't know why.

Such a commentary can easily modulate into an implied habitual meaning, as the second line of the next two suggests:

> The mist creeps over the cold grey stone,
> My girl's in Tungria; I sleep alone.

What happens habitually can seem through repetition to be something generally true. Examples may be proverbial – 'a rolling stone gathers no moss' – or they may be of the Darwinian type used regularly in *Origin of the Species* (1859) where commentary and omnetemporal truth fuse:

> We behold the face of nature bright with gladness, we often see superabundance of food; we do not see, or we forget that the birds which are idly singing around us mostly live on insects or seeds, and are thus constantly destroying life. (Beer 1996: 52–3)

The first line of Auden's poem too may be an omnetemporal/true-at-all-times statement that the wet wind blows every day and all day – that's what life is like. Its status could be on a par with Shakespeare's assertion in the second and third line of Sonnet 116: 'Love is not love / Which alters when it alteration finds'. These types even of omnetemporal/true-at-all-times assertion are time-bound but another usage is regarded by linguists as not time-bound but timeless. Examples are theological or mathematical: 'God is good'; 'Two and two make four'. These are the categories in the uses of the present tense as linguists see them: for contemporaneous commentary; future or habitual actions or events; generalizations of an omnetemporal kind and timeless truths. In practice the groups are not always distinguishable and usage may, as in Auden's poem, be ambiguous. Dogmatic assertions of a general kind come readily to the third-person narrator in *Bleak House*. He is quite sure of what is always

the effect of moonlight: 'When the moon shines very brilliantly, a soli-
tude and stillness seem to proceed from her, that influence even crowded
places full of life' (p. 748). He can ironically make omnetemporal statements about detectives and others: 'Time and place cannot bind Mr
Bucket. Like man in the abstract he is here to-day and gone to-morrow'
(p. 803); or about the elite: 'even within the stillest and politest circle,
as with the circle the necromancer draws around him, very strange appearances may be seen in active motion outside' (p. 191). And presumably without irony he can assert the fact that death by spontaneous
combustion does occur and 'it is the same death eternally' (p. 519). For
the whole range of uses it is sometimes suggested that the appropriate
umbrella term might be 'non-past tense'.

   The scope of the third-person (or omne-narrator as he may be called)
in *Bleak House* is unbounded. For what the generalizing meanings (and
possibly the habitual use) share is an assertion of authoritativeness, of a
claim by the speaker to knowledge beyond what is given by observation
in a specific instance. Consequently it follows that, contrary to expectation, the interweaving with Esther's story of a third-person narrative
using the present tense will not appear subordinate to a first-person
account which uses the past tense. Though the 'I' creates an egocentric
space and time, created and controlled by the speaker's perception (who
was perhaps an eyewitness to events), the account is inevitably time-
bound. The other narrator's account is not so bound: his utterance, by
its free-ranging nature in terms of time and its capacity for generalization, has a more comprehensive scope. The very embedding of Esther's
narrative within the omne-narrator's diminishes hers. She loses the authority of a Jane Eyre or a Lucy Snowe.

   For naturally it is the anonymous narrator who initiates the story.
He has already done so when Esther's opening remarks at the beginning of chapter three indicate her restricted horizons: 'I have a great
deal of difficulty in beginning to write my portion of these pages, for I
know I am not clever' (p. 27). A prior scenario is implied here, one
which resembles the opening of Wilkie Collins's *The Moonstone* (1868),
which is recounted by a series of first person narrators. They do so at
the dictate of a central character, Franklin Blake, who organizes the
written account of the theft and recovery of a massive and ill-fated
Indian diamond. His purpose is clear:

> In this matter of the Diamond … the characters of innocent people
> have suffered under suspicion already … The memories of innocent
> people may suffer, hereafter, for want of a record of facts to which
> those who come after us may appeal. (Trodd 1998: 7)

Each narrator is identified and all are instructed 'to write the story of
the Moonstone in turn – as far as our own personal experience extends
and no further'. Esther too has evidently been instructed to serve as a
witness and is narrating under constraint from some authority. Though
this might be assumed to be the more magisterial narrator, Esther shows
no knowledge of him except in so far as she implicitly recognizes that
there will be another 'portion' to the narrative besides her own. Her
story begins immediately after an overall survey of Chancery and its
workings and soon after she is summoned before the Lord Chancellor.
Consequently she slips, like Jo the crossing sweeper at the Inkwich,
into the role of reluctant and anxious witness.

An eyewitness in a trial is a crucial figure but this does not enhance
either Jo's or Esther's status. The evidence of a witness must be sub-
jected to scrutiny and fitted into a larger picture. It may even be dis-
counted if other evidence suggests that the witness is possibly malicious, amnesiac, a congenital liar or, like Jo, lacks understanding. The
value of evidence lies in the skill of the advocate-interpreter with a view
of the overall picture, not in the witness herself. Esther in this differs
from the witnesses in *The Moonstone*, the validity of whose accounts is
already agreed before they begin their narratives. Predetermined also is
the function of their stories: to serve as a record that will distinguish
the innocent from the guilty when gossip arises. They are not sub-
jected, as Esther implicitly is, to unceasing surveillance. Its largely silent nature does not remove the sense of pressure evident in her desire
to satisfy someone by her narrative. With Esther it is not clear what the
public object is of the case in which she is giving evidence. If she knows
of the issue at stake, she behaves as though not. The only obvious pre-
sumption about why she is constrained to tell her version of the story
would seem to be that there is a need to arrive at some factual truth.
The omne-narrator has a mission rather than a project: to enlighten
readers through the story of a quest for Lady Dedlock's secret and to
solve the mystery of Tulkinghorn's murder which arises in the course of
the search. But the story of the quest is offered as an *exemplum* not as

an end in itself like the search in *The Moonstone*. To judge from the narrator's rhetoric, the significance of the *exemplum* is what it reveals as to the state of the nation, its institutions and morals.

For Esther, by contrast, the unravelling of the mystery has a personal significance that she tries to construct by finding the true self of a narrating 'I'. Like Jane Eyre and Lucy Snowe, she is parentless, penniless and statusless. The work of construction is difficult; she has no place within a family that would offer a nominal identity. Jane Eyre at least knows that Mrs Reed is her aunt and her tormentors are her cousins. Esther is only to know Miss Barbary as a godmother, not an aunt, until the woman's death reveals her as a blood relative. It is as if she had never had parents. Her origins remain a blank: 'I had never heard my mama spoken of. I had never heard of my papa either' (p. 29). She is already 'nameless' through her illegitimacy, and the eventual discovery that her father was the nameless no-one 'Nemo' makes her doubly so. With only 'no-one' to relate to emotionally, she fetishizes her doll like Maggie Tulliver in *The Mill on the Floss*, though for different purposes, as she is later to idolize Ada Clare. The only other in her life is her virtuous godmother who potentiates her negative sense of self:

> I felt so different from her ... I felt so poor and trifling, and far off; that I never could be unrestrained with her – no; could never even love her as I wished. It made me very sorry to consider how good she was, and how unworthy of her I was; and I used ardently to hope that I might have a better heart; and I talked it over very often with the dear old doll; but I never loved my godmother as I ought to have loved her, and as I felt I must have loved her if I had been a better girl. (p. 28)

Esther's awareness of herself as an amorphous lack is given a shape or at least a label when she is told on her birthday that 'Your mother, Esther, is your disgrace and you were hers' (p. 30). The first mention of her mother coincides with the destruction of any hope of a validation for her existence, even in a past bond of affection with the one person on whom she might rely for it.

When Esther accepts the fact that the answer to 'Who am I?' is that she is her 'mother's disgrace', it is the beginning of a process that is to be repeated many times. Her identity and her path in life are appropriated by others who choose them for her. She is dispatched like a parcel, first to a school and then 'carriage free' to London by Kenge, the lawyer (p. 40). It seems that she, like the two 'wards in Jarndyce', has been adopted by John Jarndyce as his ward. But when she appears before the Lord Chancellor he rubber-stamps Jarndyce's decision to make Ada and Richard his wards and to make a gift of Esther to Ada as her 'companion'. This is later paralleled by her own receipt of the penniless daughter of a dead bailiff, Charley Coavins, as 'a present', to serve as her maid. Subsequently Esther's declassing to servant status is confirmed by the reactions of those around her at Bleak House. By a form of strikingly wordless communication the household keys are delivered to her there as an indication that she is now the housekeeper, an 'upper' servant. She is her own jailor, safely entrusted with the very keys to her own prison, which await her again after her illness. The appropriateness of her new position is pointed out by Jarndyce who tells her that she is 'clever enough to be the good little woman of our lives here … the little old woman of the Child's Rhyme' who sweeps up cobwebs. Ada and Richard accept her in this character as Dame Durden, Mother Hubbard, Mrs Shipton, Cobweb, Old Woman and Little Old Woman' (p. 121). Predictably with these and 'many names of that sort' her own name 'soon became quite lost among them'. There is an unexpected and ironic suitability in these names of nursery-tale housewives. They consign Esther, without the flattery and excitement of courtship and marriage, to a grey middle-aged domesticity. She loses other aspects of her identity when she is declassed: her youth and sexuality. All this appears later like Jarndyce's way of preparing a very young and vulnerable girl for his proposal of marriage. She is given a nominal age and an outlook suitable for the wife of a man three times her age and who is in *loco parentis*, in fulfilment of his 'old dream I sometimes dreamed when you were very young of making you my wife some day' (p. 964).

Esther's acceptance of her identity as solely a domestic resource is unquestioning. The life such an identity provides is familiar from contemporary novels: one of physically confined spaces and crowding trivia which block all other views. It is restricted to 'each little store-room, drawer and cupboard, barricaded by jams, pickles, preserves, bottles and glasses'. This environment reduces her to what she is supposed to be, 'a methodical, old-maidish sort of foolish little person' (p. 115). Like Alice in Wonderland she is suddenly physically diminished. The striking difference here from Jane Eyre, Lucy Snowe or Caroline Helstone, or Geraldine Jewsbury's eponymous Marian Withers is that she neither resents nor resists the restriction. Other fictional women do. Jane Eyre complains on behalf of such women that 'it is narrow-minded in their more privileged fellow-creatures to say that they ought to confine themselves to making puddings and knitting stockings, to playing on the piano and embroidering bags' (Mason 1996: 125–6). Caroline Helstone goes further and sees such life as 'a long slow death' (p. 451); Marian Withers, in Geraldine Jewsbury's novel of that name (1851), claims to feel 'as if I were buried alive' (3.124–5). And in her non-fictional work *Cassandra*, written in 1852, Florence Nightingale describes domestic confinement as living the life of 'a corpse, which lies motionless in its narrow bed' (Stark 1979: 51).

Esther's perception of a gap where a self might be turns her into a supreme example of feminine plasticity to the needs of others. These others fill the gap she represents with what they need. In the case of Jarndyce this is an old/young wife; for others it is the mother they lack, either in fact like Ada and Richard, or in default of a true mother like Caddy Jellyby. Esther is motherless but must herself be a true mother to those who require it. When she finally confronts the identity of her own mother in the person of Lady Dedlock her situation is unchanged. Lady Dedlock (lovingly) disowns her, telling her that:

> I must evermore consider her as dead. If I could believe that she loved me, in this agony in which I saw her, with a mother's love, she asked me to do that, for then I might think of her with greater pity imagining what she suffered. She had put herself beyond all hope, and beyond all help. Whether she preserved her secret until death, or it came to be discovered and she brought dishonour and disgrace upon the name she had taken, it was her solitary struggle always; and no affection could come near her, and no human creature could render her any aid. (p. 580)

This rejection is worse than Miss Barbary's; it is absolute. Esther's mother cannot even offer her a name but she requires unconditional maternal love from her daughter for no practical or emotional return.

Esther as usual obliges, though with a new knowledge of what it means to be her mother's disgrace. She now knows that 'it would have been better and happier for many people, if indeed I had never breathed'.

Moreover she is a source of contagion, not only an unnecessary creature but a fearsome one:

> I had a terror of myself, as the danger and possible disgrace of my own mother, and of a proud family name … I was so confused and shaken as to be possessed by a belief that it was right, and had been intended that I should die in my birth, and not intended, that I should be then alive. (p. 583)

The past clutches at Esther and draws her back into the oblivion where she feels that she really belongs, and into her time-bound prison. As a result of this shock she retreats into a state of fugue, a flight from her own identity. The immediate trigger is the sound of her footsteps on the steps below the terrace at Chesney Wold where the sound of ghostly footsteps is said to be heard when disaster threatens the Dedlock family:

> my echoing footsteps brought it suddenly into my mind that there was a dreadful truth in the legend of the Ghost's Walk; that it was I, who was to bring calamity upon the stately house; and my warning feet were haunting it even then. Seized with an augmented terror of myself which turned me cold, I ran from myself and everything. (p. 586)

The fear of self was already present – now it is terrifyingly augmented and such terrors are the only interiority that Esther reveals. They occur in dreams or abnormal states of mind when her fear of, and longing for, the void that is self to swallow her up emerges from her unconscious. It has already happened once, before the episode of the Ghost's Walk when, after kaleidoscopic and unexpected experiences in London have been thrust upon her, she falls asleep with the trusting head of Caddy Jellyby upon her knee. As she tries to 'lose' herself among the scenes of the day she literally does so by first losing the identity of the sleeper resting on her and then her own:

> Now, it was Ada; now, one of my old Reading friends from whom I could not believe that I had so recently parted. Now, it was the little mad old woman … now, someone in authority at Bleak House. Lastly, it was no one, and I was no one. (p. 63)

This loss of self is what she wished for and comes with a sense of relief. The desire to wind back the past and enter the non-existence for which she was destined becomes explicit again when the experience of a life-threatening illness brings her nearer to it. She sees a gleaming necklace strung across a great black space 'a ring, or starry circle of some kind, of which I was one of the beads'. She longs to be taken off from the necklace and be released from the 'inexplicable agony of being a part of the dreadful thing' (p. 556).

These trance-like states parallel those of Lucy Snowe in *Villette* though they are very differently handled by Esther. Writing of *Villette*, Shuttleworth says that in nineteenth-century psychology 'Hallucinations ... were classically regarded as signs of madness'; and in psychic economy 'as in the economics of the period, self-control was the watchword of the moral managers' (Shuttleworth 1996: 221). Esther has no sense of a stable self, such as Lucy Snowe develops, to exert control: the emergence of these hallucinatory states is triggered by emotional experiences that she cannot process – hence the masculine idea of rational self-control belongs to the omne-narrator. Esther's glimpses of her own interiority as a precipitous chasm elicit the strongest desire she ever reveals – for annihilation. Nightingale describes this as what domestic claustrophobia ultimately induces. She imagines the dying words of a woman confined as Esther is: 'Oh! if you know how gladly I leave this life, how much courage I feel to take the chance of another, than of anything I see before me in this, you would put on your wedding clothes instead of mourning for me' (Stark, 1979: 54).

Esther's perception of herself also as a dangerous source of contagion which would be best extinguished arises from Lady Dedlock's illicit sexuality and the destructive power which it has through her own survival. The contamination threatens her own sanity, the honour of a stately house and her mother's name. As the product of a tainted sexuality, Esther can pass on the taint. Her mother's revelation therefore leaves her doubly debarred from sexual love, for she is already barred once by her desexualized role of 'little Old Woman'. She implements the prohibition herself by marginalizing her prospective suitor Woodcourt. For over twenty chapters she prefers to make only oblique references to 'a gentleman of a dark complexion – a young surgeon' (p. 214); 'a medical gentleman who was so good as to attend Miss Flite' (p. 232). It is only belatedly, after his shipwreck and heroism on a journey to the East Indies, that she admits a potentially closer relationship now happily precluded:

> I *had thought*, sometimes, that Mr Woodcourt loved me; and that *if he had been richer*, he would perhaps have told me that he loved me, before he went away. I *had thought*, sometimes, that if he had done so, I should have been glad of it. But, how much better it was now, that this had never happened! (p. 570)

Woodcourt's love is carefully presented as already past for those in the past by the use of the pluperfect tense. Even there, it is rendered remote as merely a speculation of Esther's that only occurred 'sometimes'. Her possible response to his affection is rendered even more distant as, in addition to being a (past) speculation, it involves two hypotheses. First, that if Woodcourt had been richer he might have declared the love which she sometimes (but not always) thought that he possibly (though not certainly) felt. Second, that if being richer he had expressed his love, she might possibly (though not certainly) have been glad. This is very reminiscent of Arthur Clennam's account of his (non) feelings for Pet Meagles in *Little Dorrit* (1857): 'If Clennam had not decided against falling in love with Pet; if he had the weakness to do it; … he would have been, that night, unutterably miserable … As it was, the rain fell heavily, drearily' (chapter 18). Such emotions as these are, as he reminds himself, 'Nobody's state of mind' and like Esther it is with Nobody that he identifies himself.

The refusal to allow Woodcourt to enter the text figures her inability to let him penetrate her life. For Jane Eyre and Lucy Snowe passionate desire carves a way out of a claustrophobic domesticity. With Esther, her desires are displaced onto the doll-figure of Ada Clare, as earlier they had been displaced onto her actual doll. It is on Ada that she lavishes expressions of affection in the discourse of conventional romantic novels. She uses the language that a male lover of Ada might use in such a text: 'my darling', 'my beauty', 'my angel girl'. Ada is her main concern when she catches the deadly fever: how can she keep Ada from infection? Charley is expected to nurse her, and in doing so contracts the disease, but that to Esther is no disaster. Not only her language but her feelings are those of a lover. How can she endure their separation? Will Ada still love her when she finds her so disfigured by pock-marks? The culmination of these intense fears is their climactic reunion:

> I did not mean to do it, but I ran upstairs to my room, and hid myself behind the door. There I stood, trembling, even when I heard

my darling calling as she came up-stairs … She ran in … Ah, my
angel girl! the old dear look, all love, all fondness, all affection.
Nothing else in it – no, nothing, nothing!

O how happy I was, down upon the floor, with my sweet beautiful girl down upon the floor too, holding my scarred face to her
lovely cheek, bathing it with tears and kisses … calling me by every
tender name that she could think of, and pressing me to her faithful
heart. (p. 588)

Esther's uncertain identity becomes still more blurred: already declassed,
devalued, desexualized, and prematurely aged; she is now resexualized
in a different gender. Her surrogate status as mother, daughter, lover to
Ada encapsulates her willingness to adopt whatever role others create
for her. She is the perfect example of Florence Nightingale's biting summary of the treatment of women by the family they belong to: it 'uses
people *not* for what they are but for what it wants them for – for its
own uses. It thinks of them not as what God has made them but as
something which *it* has arranged that they shall be' (Stark 1979: 37,
original emphasis).

In domestic ideology, and later for Darwin in the natural universe,
adaptation was a wonderful mechanism. By contrast, in *Bleak House* it
represents systemic social distortion. Esther, under pressures from society, adapts herself to the wishes and needs of those around her. As a
result her uncertain sense of self atrophies or appears only in malign
shapes. The consequent suppression of desire causes it to be diverted
from Woodcourt to Ada, creating a disturbing asymmetry in the narrative structure. The central concern of Esther's narrative, one apparently
fulfilled by her final union with Woodcourt, is strangely off-centred.
The imbalance becomes even more acute when, in an elaborately extended sequence with Esther at her most disfigured and vulnerable,
John Jarndyce proposes to her. He does this by hinting that he has
something important to say to her but will only do so in a letter which
she must first ask for. This is typical of Esther's convoluted existence in
which, as both performer and critic of her own performance, she finds
herself playing a game without knowing the rules. In this ultimate manipulation Jarndyce constrains her to become both his dutiful ward
and his dutiful wife by telling her not to act out of a sense of duty. She
must not only submit and appear to choose by collecting the letter but
tell herself that she is not submitting. Jarndyce's stance as he forces her

to perceive, it is that of a man who refuses to exert any kind of pressure to secure what he wants. In practice it has become clear that, like William Dorrit, he lives a fantasy in which he carefully protects himself from recognizing the significance of actions, such as taking Skimpole at face value, and exercising a painlessly self-gratifying philanthropy, as well as proposing to a penniless young dependent. Yet structurally he is placed to be the lynchpin of the unworldly domesticity and selflessness which is the only beacon in the naughty world of Chancery, Tom-all-alone's, Tulkinghorn and the Smallweeds. The distortion of the narrative progression is compounded as Esther's expression of desire is diverted to Ada, and her sexual commitment to Jarndyce. This structural enactment of distortion is more powerful than Nightingale's troping of the warping effect that domestic life had upon her by the figure of the bound feet of Chinese women.

At the same time, the unravelling of the plot, instead of revealing the significance of Esther's narrative and her relevance as a witness in the unnamed law case, only serves to show the unnecessary nature of her supposedly crucial evidence. She was selected from the many persons involved to tell her story in the first person and undertook it as an awesome duty. But why is it necessary? Because Esther has a crucial role in the solving of the mystery or mysteries? But the discovery and revelation of Lady Dedlock's guilty secret is effected by Tulkinghorn, Guppy, Smallweed and finally Inspector Bucket. Because she can help solve the mystery of Tulkinghorn's murder? But Bucket does that efficiently. Because she is to be the wife of the deus ex machina Jarndyce? But in the end she isn't. In Hogg's *The Private Memoirs and Confessions of a Justified Sinner* the first person narrative follows that of the third person. It is told by the man who is the focus of attention in both narratives: the murderer of his elder brother. It acts to cast doubt on the apparently 'factual' account of the first narrative and creates uncertainty as to whether the first-person narrator Wringhim was truly possessed by the devil or only believed himself to be. Both hollow out the other narrative and each is integral to its significance of the other. Each account comments on the other and relates to it organically.

The relationship between the two narratives in *Bleak House* is very different. As already indicated, the omne-narrator is as authoritative as Darwin in his use of the present tense. His use of the third person is itself a claim to objectivity. Where Esther's space is claustrophobic, his view of space is panoramic. The opening God's eye view of London in fog ranges to Kent in the south and Essex in the north. In language reminiscent of the flood in the Book of Genesis he creates what he sees in a string of verbless nominals:

> London ... Implacable November weather. As much mud in the streets, as if the *waters had but newly retired from the face of the earth* ... Smoke lowering down from chimney-pots, making a soft black drizzle ... Dogs, indistinguishable in mire ... Horses, scarcely better; splashed to their very blinkers. Foot passengers ...
>
> Fog everywhere. Fog up the river, where it flows among green aits and meadows; fog down the river, where it rolls defiled among the tiers of shipping, and the waterside pollutions of a great (and dirty) city. Fog on the Essex marshes, fog on the Kentish heights. (p. 13)

The omne-narrator also ranges over time. He goes back to prehistory with the reference to an imagined 'Megalosaurus, forty feet long or so, waddling like an elephantine lizard up Holborn Hill.' He moves forward to the end of history in describing 'flakes of soot ... as big as full-grown snow-flakes – gone in mourning, one might imagine for the death of the sun' (p. 13). Esther's space is confined to what she can see, her time to past events at which she was present. The omne-narrator is not so restricted but can see all time and physical space as continuums to be commented on as a commentator does on a football match. This allows him to juggle with both in a way inaccessible to Esther who can record only a single chronological sequence. The omne-narrator, seeing all time as 'present' before him, can disrupt it. Having told of Bucket's revelation to Sir Leicester about his wife's past, he can revert to an earlier time:

> Inspector Bucket of the Detective has not yet struck his great blow as just now chronicled, but is yet refreshing himself with sleep preparatory to his field-day, when, through the night and along the freezing wintry roads a chaise and pair comes out of Lincolnshire making its way towards London. (p. 839)

Unlike Esther, this narrator requires no coaches for travel. He can survey the Dedlocks' place in Lincolnshire from the Ghost's Walk to the stables. He can follow the journey of the Dedlocks as they travel from

Paris to London, and precede one or other of them from the town house to the country.

The omne-narrator's grand view of time and space translates into a penetrating range of knowledge and understanding. Whereas Esther has no knowledge of him, he knows more about her than she does about herself. It is his narrative in which Mrs Chadband is revealed as the servant of the aunt who brought Esther up and who can tell the story of her birth; that Guppy reveals to Lady Dedlock that her illegitimate child is alive not dead at birth; that Bucket tells Sir Leicester about his wife's past. It is implicit in his version that he knows the whole story from beginning to end and in all its details. Esther, like everyone else in the text, is under his constant surveillance and she is only performing an allotted task.

Others in the text have problems with reading and documents but everything is an open book to him and he can extract every trace of significance from what he sees, including these characters' lack of language. Neither Krook nor Jo can read and their illiteracy is a measure of their isolation. Krook lusts to read documents which he imagines would reveal a lucrative secret and, failing, suffers a solitary death fuelled by his own gin-drinking. Jo, an Esther-figure, is similarly cut off from human society. The omne-narrator can understand both why Krook struggles desperately to read, and how Jo's lack of reading affects him:

> It must be a strange state to be like Jo. To shuffle through the streets, unfamiliar with the shapes, and in utter darkness as to the meaning, of those mysterious symbols, so abundant over the shops, at the corners of streets, and on the doors, and in the windows! To see people read, and to see people write ... and not, to have the least idea of all that language – to be, to every scrap of it, stone blind and dumb! (p. 257)

This draws on a view of human language (as a feature of distinguishing human beings from animals) that was losing ground in the contemporary debate on language, though it was still being asserted ten years later by the controversial philologist Max Müller: 'Man speaks and no brute has ever uttered a word. Language is our Rubicon, and no brute will dare to cross it' (Dowling 1982: 173). The omne-narrator accepts this conservative opinion that without a grasp of language Jo sees 'horses, dogs, and cattle go by me, and to know that in my ignorance I belong to them, and not to the superior beings in my shape that I offend!' (p 258). This undermines the social criticism assumed to be implicit in the picture of Jo's life and Tom-all-Alone's.

I have referred throughout to the omne-narrator as 'he' not because I take the term to be gender-neutral but because it is gender specific. If the third-person narrator, with all space-time 'present' before him, is God-like, then God is undoubtedly male. This is made plain in nineteenth-century terms by his knowledge of worlds beyond Esther's domesticity: by his confident grasp of such masculine spheres as those of law and politics. Observing these over long stretches of time he has watched repeated patterns of behaviour and events that can be generically described, in Darwin's way, by the use of the present tense with habitual reference: Chancery goings-on may be Byzantine in their complexity but he has seen them many times before:

> On such an afternoon, some score of members of the High Court of Chancery bar ought to be – as here they are – mistily engaged in one of the ten thousand stages of an endless cause, tripping one another up on slippery precedents, groping knee-deep in technicalities ... This is the Court of Chancery; which has its decaying houses, and its blighted lands in every shire; which has its worn-out lunatic in every mad-house; and its dead in every churchyard; ... which gives to monied might the means abundantly of wearying out the right; which so exhausts finances, patience, courage, hope; and so overthrows the brain and breaks the heart. (pp. 14–15)

The same repetition of patterns as in Chancery is recorded in political activities on behalf of the Coodleites and Boodleites who alternate endlessly in governing the country. These linguistically and politically equivalent parties go in and out of office. Their indistinguishable supporters such as Sir Leicester's relatives and hangers-on are, like those in Chancery, represented as a generic group performing generic actions. When Sir Leicester returns to his country place, 'down come the cousins and others from all points in the compass' (p. 642) for though 'the cousins generally are rather shy of Chesney Wold in its dullness', they 'take to it a little in the shooting season' (p. 984). At a General Election they act as a species in Sir Leicester's interest for Coodleites (or Doodleites):

> Daily the cousins trot through dust, and canter over roadside turf,
> away to hustings and polling booths (with leather gloves and hunt-
> ing-whips for the counties, and kid gloves and riding canes for the
> boroughs), and daily bring back reports on which Sir Leicester holds
> forth after dinner. (p. 643)

For this narrator, as has been pointed out, the Jarndyce–Dedlock–
Tulkinghorn story is an exemplum of society's state. Its significance is
drawn out in answer to the narrator's rhetorical questions which focus
the issues involved. They relate to society at large and the ruling classes
in particular – 'your Majesty, … my Lords and gentlemen … Right
Reverends and Wrong Reverends … men and women born with Heavenly compassion in your hearts' (p. 734). The central question is Darwin's question, the one implicit in a multi-plot, multi-peopled novel:
how do all these things and people relate? It is triggered by the proximity of Jo, the crossing sweeper, to the Dedlocks' grand townhouse with
its Mercuries/footmen hanging their heavily powdered heads 'like overblown sun-flowers' (p. 735): 'What connexion can there be, between
the place in Lincolnshire, the house in town, the Mercury in powder,
and the whereabout of Jo the outlaw with the broom?' But this is not a
question merely about individuals, as its amplification makes clear:
'What connexion can there have been between many people in the
innumerable histories of this world, who, from opposite sides of great
gulfs, have, nevertheless been very curiously brought together?' (p. 256).
The phrase 'great gulfs' does not refer to oceans but is the expression
characteristically used in fiction of the period for the gap between rich
and poor, exemplified by the story of Dives the rich man and Lazarus
the beggar alluded to in Elizabeth Gaskell's *Mary Barton* (1848) and
North and South (1855), and Geraldine Jewsbury's *Marian Withers*
(1851), as well as in several ballads (Smith 1980: 15). It is used in
Shirley (1848) by Caroline Helstone's mother, Mrs Pryor, who speaks
of the 'great gulf' between her daughter's class and the workman,
William Farren's.

What Jo represents in this question of the connection between him and the
upper classes is figured by the description of Tom-all-Alone's which is placed
just after the narrator's formulation of his central question:

> Jo lives – that is to say Jo has not yet died, in a ruinous place, known
> to the like of him as Tom-all-Alone's. It is a black, dilapidated street,

avoided by all decent people; where the crazy houses were seized upon, when their decay was far advanced, by some bold vagrants, who, after establishing their own possession, took to letting them out in lodgings. Now, these tumbling tenements contain by night, a swarm of misery. As, on the ruined human wretch, vermin parasites appear, so, these ruined shelters have bred a crowd of foul existence that crawls in and out of gaps in walls and boards; and coils itself to sleep, in maggot numbers. (pp. 256–7)

The question then is how to view the great gulf that exists between the inhabitants of Tom-all-Alone's and those of the Dedlocks' houses. It is the question 'between property and labour' to which Thackeray could not find the end; the one which Carlyle earlier phrased simply 'Is the condition of the English working people wrong?'; the one which caused Disraeli in *Sybil* (1845) to give it the subtitle 'The Two Nations', referring to the rich and the poor.

Since the omne-narrator's question here is rhetorical he provides his own answers. First he incorporates a literally accurate answer into the description of the inhabitants of Tom-all-Alone's. The 'foul existence' that lives there 'comes and goes, fetching and carrying fever, and sowing more evil in its every footprint than Lord Doodle and Sir Thomas Coodle, and the Duke of Foodle, and all the fine gentlemen in office, down to Zoodle shall set right in five hundred years – though born expressly to do it' (pp. 256–7). Physical infection makes all humanity kin and this threat is fulfilled as Jo infects first Charley and then Esther who might infect Boodle, Coodle, Doodle, or even Zoodle. But this is not a complete account of the connection between the classes, though it is similar to the more extended one which follows much later and also combines what is repugnant with what is a fearful threat. Tom, the narrator says, is going to perdition with no-one to put him right:

> But he has his revenge. Even the winds are his messengers and they serve him in these hours of darkness. There is not a drop of Tom's corrupted blood but propagates infection and contagion somewhere. It shall pollute this very night the choice stream … of a Norman house, and his Grace shall not be able to say Nay to the infamous alliance. (p. 710)

The description echoes Dickens' speech on the need for improvements in sanitation to the Metropolitan Sanitary Association in May

1851, also using the present tense of authoritative assertion:

> That no one can estimate the amount of mischief which is grown in dirt; that no one can say here it stops, or there it stops ... is as certain as it is that the air from Gin Lane will be carried when the wind is easterly, into Mayfair, or that a vigorous pestilence raging furiously in St Giles's, no mortal list of Lady Patronesses can keep out of Almack's. (Fielding 1960: 128)

The bodily economy figures the city, as Connor points out (Connor 1996: 215). The two, body and city, become indistinguishable as the title of the French visitor to London, Flora Tristran (1803–44), indicates by the chapter in her *London Journal* (1840) which names it 'The Monster City'. Space and orientation are crucial aspects of the description: deixis becomes an overriding figure. Tristran contrasts the 'superb' West End with its 'well built' houses, 'nicely laid out' streets, 'dazzling carriages', 'magnificently attired ladies', dandies on magnificent horses, with the 'south and north-east of the city ... where workers, prostitutes and a swarm of rootless individuals live – people reduced to vagrancy through unemployment or vice, or forced by poverty and starvation to beg, thieve or murder' (Hawkes 1982: 19). Tristran's account makes clear both the ease of the extension of corruption from bodily to the psychic economy and the uncertainty as to which is prior unemployment or vice.

Certainly the contagion of Tom's plague spreading silently from red blood to blue ('polluted' to 'choice') is moral as well as physical. It threatens the spread of 'obscenity ... degradation ... ignorance ... wickedness ... brutality ... [to] work its retribution, through every order of society up to the proudest of the proud and highest of the high' (p. 710). The 'brutality' and 'violence' include the danger that Sir Leicester feared might be behind threats against the 'fine, slow British' institution of Chancery. Such protests could 'encourage some person in the lower classes to rise up somewhere – like Wat Tyler', leader of the Peasants' Revolt in 1381.

In general terms the omne-narrator's answer to the question of the connection between rich and poor is that the poor, though greatly to be pitied, threaten disease, depravity and insurrection which will affect the rich. Their pitiable state is in his description linguistically subordinated, a parenthesis embedded within the threat. The Jehovah-narrator moves at this point from compassion to expediency as a motive for getting 'Tom' to go right. Given his prophetic stance, this begins to sound like his threat of divine thunderbolts.

The move in this account from physical to moral disease is easily figured by the proximity of filth, disease and prostitution to drunkenness and crime. Since they are merely listed in the prophecy of Tom's revenge, their causal connection is never made clear. It is possible to interpret the passage as making poverty the root of all these evils. But if so, then why is Jo, the representative of the Tom-all-Aloners (St Giles), miraculously immune like Oliver Twist from the moral evils of obscenity, wickedness and brutality? Like Esther, his alter ego, he is ignorant but his ignorance appears to be an isolation that insulates him and becomes a condition of his innocence. Corruption is much more readily found among the Guppies and the Smallweeds.

The secondary question asked by the narrator refers to the nature not of the East End but the West. Tristran describes this as the home of 'the high aristocracy, the genteel professions ... the provincial nobility' (Hawkes 1982: 19). These precisely make up the 'brilliant and distinguished circle' which assembles at Chesney Wold pursued by 'the fashionable intelligence' (p. 188). They have, it is said, some measure of 'education, sense, courage, honour, and beauty, and virtue' (though only the last but one of these is made evident to the reader). But for all this, the narrator senses 'something a little wrong about it, in despite of its immense advantages. What can it be?' (p. 188). The hypotheses that are considered as possible answers to this question satirize topical opinions among the upper classes. These include the view of politicians like Lansdowne, Russell and Stanley, who according to *The Times* of 5 March 1851, were 'wonderfully agreed about the small number of men at all fit, or likely, for power' (Butt and Tillotson 1968: 188). But allusion is also made to Disraeli's romantic view in *Coningsby* (1845), which is perhaps a variant on such politicians' that the two nations of rich and poor can be turned into one by reinstating distinctions of rank and transforming the working classes into a loyal 'peasantry'. Their loyalty will be rewarded by a reciprocal paternalism on the part of a fatherly aristocracy (vol. 3, chapter 3). This is what Dickens calls 'putting back the hands upon the Clock of Time, and cancelling a few hundred years of history' to make 'the Vulgar very picturesque and faithful' (p. 189).

Both these sets of opinion, however, are inadequate answers to the question of what is to keep society stable and united. They merely offer costumes for inequity to perform in. The Dedlocks, Boodles, Buffys (like Lansdowne, Russell, Stanley and Disraeli) do not inhabit the real world of East and West End; they are 'great actors for whom the stage is reserved' (pp. 190–1).

On this stage they are preoccupied by performing the social rituals of dining, dancing, dress, entertaining, hunting, and sycophancy, summarized by the narrator under the headings of various forms of 'Dandyism'. In terms of the real world they are idle and inert. Their great defect is that they have 'found out the perpetual stoppage' (p. 189), the 'do-nothingism' that Carlyle castigates and that occupies the Circumlocution Office in *Little Dorrit*. They deal with the need that 'Tom shall be set right' only through suppression by 'constable, or by beadles, or by bell-ringing, or by force of figures, or by high church, or by low church, or by no church or by stonebreaking' (p. 710). This inertia and hierarchical order is rebuked in the judicial summing up on Jo's death: 'Dead, your Majesty; dead, my lords and gentlemen. Dead, Right Reverends and Wrong Reverends of every order. Dead, men and women born with Heavenly compassion in your hearts and dying thus around us every day' (p. 734). Acting in the role of judge and jury at this informal inquest, the omne-narrator turns his addressees into defendants accused of causing death by lack of compassion. His gesture of apparent willingness to be accused himself by the use of an inclusive 'us' in 'dying thus around us' is more play-acting. His tirade, like others earlier, demonstrates the very 'Heavenly compassion' that they are accused of lacking and which occludes him from their category. The rhetorical 'us' is a familiar (not to be taken seriously) inadequacy trope. To assert that *we* all need to cultivate compassion is a polite use of the pronoun simply used to avoid the condemnatory force of using 'you'.

This self-insulation by rhetorical distress does not survive the metatext which arises from the combination of the omne-narrator's narrative with Esther's. In this new universe of discourse there are only two participants: the two narrators who survey the other characters. As with the multiplot story, this juxtaposition already poses the question that the two accounts raise internally as to the rich and the poor, the powerful and the weak. What is their connection? Is it a benign and equal relationship? Many structural as well as verbal things combine to make clear that the answer is negative.

The very embedding of Esther's story within that of the omne-narrator already suggests a power hierarchy. This is reinforced by Esther's confinement within a past which is for him part of a long continuum. Temporal and spatial imperialism readily equates with power; spatial and temporal restriction indicates weakness. It is at this point that the unnecessary nature of Esther's narrative becomes relevant. Its signifi-cance in the broader account is not made any clearer by its relationship to the other narrative. It originally combines the impetus of the com-mand to bear witness and a personal and illicit desire to find out who she is. This urgency is lost when the discovery of her parentage fails to answer the question. Multiple identities are already imposed on her by others and continued to be until her last words which close the novel:

> But I know that my dearest little pets are very pretty, and that my darling is very beautiful, and that my husband is very handsome, and that my guardian has the brightest and most benevolent face that ever was seen; and that they can very well do without much beauty in me – even supposing – (p. 989)

She is still only a kaleidoscopic mirror of those around her – mother, wife and ward for them. Where she might arrive at a self in the final clause there is only an unfinished sentence, a gap, a lack, an absence. Unlike Jane Eyre, Lucy Snowe and David Copperfield, she is in the same state at the end of her story as at the beginning. She cannot con-trol circumstances: they control her. Her personal enterprise has failed; her public task that was imposed on her has turned her from witness to prisoner. Narrative has become an ordeal which traps her in the past, obliging her to relive in detail a wretched childhood, the discovery of shameful illegitimacy, parental rejection and finally a painful test im-posed on her by Jarndyce. By a manipulation supposed to increase her delighted gratitude and his self-gratification, he makes her believe that he is arranging their marriage at a time when he knows that she and Woodcourt love each other.

He is careful never to lie but only to deceive by referring to Bleak House and its mistress, which she takes to be his house, while he knows that Woodcourt too will own a replica of Bleak House. He is careful to omit no turn of the screw. He gives her money to buy the necessary clothes and she gets full marks for ordering her wardrobe to please his taste. He sends for her to follow him to Yorkshire, allegedly to approve 'the unpretending and suitable place' he has prepared for her lover. Esther claims to recognize his kindness and sobs at it. But even she has to allow that her tears are ambiguous: 'When I went to bed, I cried. I am bound to confess that I cried; but I hope it was with pleasure, though I am not quite sure that it was with pleasure' (p. 962). She browbeats herself into blindness to his cruelty by repeating twice over the words of Jarndyce's proposal of marriage. The last ordeal is her view of the miniature Bleak House decorated and furnished according to all her 'little tastes and fancies' (p. 963). Only after all these tests does Jarndyce end the torment by revealing that he has not only chosen a new home for her but a different husband – Woodcourt. All major decisions have been taken for her and she can safely be handed over to the new surveillance of her doctor-lover. She is left in mid-sentence to become the doll in 'quite a rustic cottage of dolls' rooms' with 'little rustic verandah doors, and underneath the tiny wooden colonnades' (pp. 962–3). The diminishing effect of her entry into the first Bleak House when she was declassed, de-sexed and aged, is replicated and she is grateful to enter the smaller prison.

This is in the universe of discourse represented by her own text. In that of the metatext, subordinated spatially, temporally and psychically to the omne-narrator, she is similarly put through 'tests' by whoever instructed her to write her 'portion of these pages'. The double structure of a novel with two narrators, one of whom is unidentified, raises the question of who he is. In *The Confessions of a Justified Sinner* the third-person narrator is identified as 'the editor'. In default of a label and a failure to offer an identification, a parallel becomes evident, suggested by the many which criss-cross the novel: Krook and the Lord Chancellor, Skimpole and Richard, Tulkinghorn and Bucket, Esther and her doll, Esther and Charley, Esther and the brickmaker's baby, Esther and Jo the outcasts. There is a similarity of authority and manipulativeness between the omne-narrator and Jarndyce, who always knows more than he tells. The parallel reinforces the implication that, like Jarndyce, it is the omne-narrator who in the metatext subjects Esther to an emotionally excruciating ordeal whose only function is to circulate Esther among the men around her and finally stop her after a circular journey from Bleak House to a miniature Bleak House. The omne-narrator's relation to Esther enacts the relation of society to Jo and Tom-all-Alone's which for all the rhetorical protestations is one of control and suppression. Esther is trapped both in her doll's house and, in the metatext, in a larger unknown narrative, and it is her confinement to the present tense and the telling only of what she knows first-hand that constitute the walls of her prison.

Negatives

6

Maiden no more:
negative values in *Tess of the d'Urbervilles*

Negation one might say is a gesture of exclusion. But such a
gesture is used in a variety of cases. (Wittgenstein)

IT is true that negation is an indication of exclusion but as the ambiguous word 'gesture' suggests, its potential is greater than a mere
capacity to draw a cross over a statement by denying it. In fact a gesture
may be a misleading sign of which the meaning is contrary to what it
might indicate – a 'mere gesture': 'Oh no, I couldn't impose on you like
that!' In *Tess of the d'Urbervilles* (1891) negatives are a prominent feature of the text. They are used pointedly by the narrator and are Tess's
characteristic form of speech. The work itself is structured on an attempt to transform a negative 'impure' into 'pure'.

The potential of negative use in English is large. The study of language acquisition has shown child learners acquiring the ability to express four kinds of negation: non-existence – 'No biscuit!'; rejection –
'No milk!'; non-compliance – 'No bed!'; denial – 'No bad boy!'. 'No' in
these structures is clearly polyvalent as it is in more complex forms of
language. Further, beyond these primitive examples, context can alter
the significance of a negative statement: it may range from a heartfelt
denial of guilt to a polite refusal made out of courtesy. In the first three
Phases of the text, Tess makes frequent use of non-compliant negatives,
first to Alec d'Urberville and then to Angel Clare. But the force of
these expressions is very different depending on which of them she is
addressing.

There are also various ways of expressing negation in addition to negative forms like *no, not, nor, neither, none, nobody, no-one*. There are many lexical items such as *deny, reject, refuse, refute, contradict, disprove, invalidate; impure, unreal, illogical, implausible, unwarranted;* and *minus, without, except*.

Some of the complexities of negative usage can be described as variations on scope/domain; or in emphasis. The first of these, the area covered by negation will be discussed in relation to *Little Dorrit* (chapter 7). The second is the fact that the possibility exists of indicating extra emphasis. To clarify this, it must be pointed out first that in current English emphasis in a given context is frequently associated with the longer of two possible forms (known as the extended one). An instance would be that to the native speaker 'Who's been eating my porridge?' is more emphatically indignant than 'Who's eaten my porridge?', though in both cases the bowl is evidently empty. Similarly a meaningless dummy word makes 'Not bloody likely!' a more emphatic refusal than 'Not likely!' In earlier English, multiple negative forms within a single utterance could add similar emphasis. Shakespeare's 'You may deny that you were not the cause', contains two negatives: *deny* = 'say not' and *not*. But it is really a forceful way of saying 'You may well say that you were not the cause'. In written English with the exception of for instance, 'I *shouldn't* be surprised if it *didn't* rain' meaning 'I should be surprised if it did not rain', multiple negatives are no longer used to add emphasis.

Instead mere repetition of the negative particle, roughly equivalent to the extended forms discussed above, is the way of making a negative utterance emphatic: for example '*No! No! No!* I *didn't* do it.' An extreme example of such repetition is found in George Herbert's prayer-poem 'Sighs and Groans' which pleads for God's mercy. Its purport is indicated by the first line: 'O do not use me after my sins ...' In each stanza the first and last lines are paired as follows:

{O do not use me ...
{O do not bruise me.

{O do not urge me ...
{O do not scourge me.

{O do not blind me ...
{O do not grind me.

{O do not fill me ...
{O do not kill me.

By contrast it is possible to use a repeated negative pattern as a way of defining a positive in a way that makes negation a mere gesture. Tennyson's poem 'Marion' offers a simple example:

Thou art not handsome, art not plain
and thou dost own no graceful art.
Yet thou dost hold an ample reign
within the human heart.

What starts as a mildly disparaging account of the woman leads to a positive conclusion by ruling out other possibilities. Since Marion is neither beautiful nor graceful, the fact that she is a queen of hearts must mean that she has some other surpassing quality. A more arithmetically effective example of the same kind is found in Sonnet 55 of Edmund Spenser's *Amoretti* on his cruel mistress (my emphasis):

So ofte as I her beauty doe behold,
And therewith do her cruelty compare,
I marvaile of what substance was the mould
The which her made attonce so cruell faire.

Not earth; for her high thoughts more heavenly are,
not water; for her love doth burne like fyre:
not ayre; for she is not so light or rare,
not fyre; for she doth friese with faint desire.

This systematically rules out in turn each of the four elements on which all matter was supposed to be based. It thus allows Spenser to conclude triumphantly that these exclusions leave only one heavenly possibility:

Then needs another Element inquire
Wherof she mote be made: that is the skye.

Like Tennyson's negatives, Spenser's are mere gestures which serve to make the final assertion more flatteringly forceful. So negatives can be deployed to assert positive values.

Hardy's most controversial novel adopts those multiple uses of the negatives as its distinctive mode. In this context the project of *Tess* to attach positive value to the negative concept of impurity in a woman seems less strange. In contemporary terms Tess was plainly impure, the opposite of a pure woman as then understood. This makes the subtitle *A Pure Woman* apparently contradictory since it directs readers to interpret the text as the portrait of 'a pure woman faithfully presented'. Hardy spelt out the meaning of his subtitle in his Preface to the 1912 Wessex edition of his narrative:

> It was appended at the last moment, after reading the final proofs, as being the estimate left in a candid mind of the heroine's character – an estimate no one was likely to dispute. It was disputed more than anything else in the book.

The conventional response to this audacity, however, might have been anticipated with certainty. It took forceful forms. R. H. Hutton in his review of the novel in the *Spectator* of January 1892 demanded to know how the word pure could possibly be applied to the heroine. 'She was pure enough in her instincts ... But she had no deep sense of fidelity to those instincts' (Cox 1970: 193). Hutton has at least grasped the argument of Hardy's text which resembles Tennyson's logic in his 'Marion' poem. Tess is not pure in the usual sense of the word which is based on too shallow a view. But she is represented as a heroine who is supremely moral and who therefore deserves the adjective 'pure' since that is the highest accolade for a woman at this time. The usual sense of the word is based on an assessment of women in terms of their sexual status. They can only be pure if they are 'chaste': either what Hardy calls 'an unsullied virgin' or a chaste (i.e. faithful) and overtly sexless wife who is mother rather than sexual partner. The contrasting titles of the first two Phases of the narrative deliberately follow up the subtitle's assertion that Tess is pure by headlining the fact that 'The Maiden' (= virgin) is now 'Maiden No More' (= fornicator). For the contemporary reader these titles were equivalent to 'Pure Woman' and 'Impure Woman'. This conventional judgement is again pointed up in the episode where Tess has left home but is recognized by a Marlott man who knows her story. When his companion calls her 'A comely maid', the narrator records his reaction '"True – comely enough. But unless I make a mistake -" and he negatived the remainder of the definition forthwith' (p. 295).

Hardy had set himself a difficult task linguistically by locking his text in his title and subtitle into the terminology of conventions about women which then prevailed. A single individual cannot change the common and specific meaning of a word (such as *pure*) at will. Furthermore he adds to his difficulties by making Tess doubly 'impure' in contemporary terms. Not content with showing her losing her virginity when unmarried, he later reveals her as an adulterous wife. He piles on the negatives: she is not a chaste virgin and not a chaste wife. Almost as a demonstration that no raw act is the measure of morality, the narrative goes to extremes. Tess is represented not only as conventionally 'evil' in sexual terms but in the most extreme of actions when she stabs Alec. Having done this, Hardy spells out in his letters his own conviction that his heroine was essentially pure, purer than many a so-called unsullied virgin, and above 'the parochial British understanding' which 'knock itself against this word [pure] like a humblebee against a wall, not seeing that "paradoxical morality" may have a great deal to say for itself, especially in a work of fiction' (Purdy and Millgate 1979: 267). His project broadly then is to turn a negative into a positive and do so by showing that the moral value of an individual resides in something other than a superficial assessment of their actions according to a set of rigid rules. The idea of a more profound judgement is outlined in the comments on Angel Clare that, as he begins 'to discredit the old appraisements of morality', he recognizes that 'The beauty or ugliness of a character lay not only in its achievements, but in its aims and impulses; its true history lay not among things done, but among things willed' (p. 462). With this characteristically negative formulation (not A but B; not C but D), the overt project of the text is emphatically asserted.

Hardy confronts this problem head-on using all the resources of fiction. Earlier defences of fallen women were by no means radical and did not challenge the common language in the way that *Tess* does. Their strategies can be illustrated by Elizabeth Gaskell's *Ruth* (1848) and George Gissing's *The Unclassed* (1884). Both novels deal with their heroines' sexual impurity by sanitizing it and by endowing them with the middle-class virtues of self-sacrifice, altruism and domestic efficiency. Ruth is seduced at a tender age and then abandoned with her illegitimate child. She repents utterly, accepting her impurity; and uses her life and death (from fever contracted while nursing) to atone for it. Ida Starr takes up a life of prostitution, strangely, to avoid the sexual predatoriness of her employers when working as a servant. In a convoluted way she takes up prostitution to avoid impurity. Neither she nor Ruth show signs of sexual feeling and both are the epitome of domestic rectitude.

But Hardy's narrative makes a point of stressing Tess's sexuality in sharp contrast to these earlier narratives. Her sexual allure, that conventional sign of deviance in a woman, is something that all the men in the text, Alex, Angel and the narrator, respond to. It has often been pointed out that her sexualized body is frequently referred to in the notorious allusions to her 'mobile peony mouth' – a phrase bowdlerized in the serialized version in the *Graphic* magazine to her 'peony cheek'. The need for the bowdlerizing is made clear by the then current physiognomical interpretation of human eyes and ears as 'intellectual organs', and nose and mouth as 'animal organs'. Prominence of either of the latter two features, such as fullness of lip in the black races, were supposed to indicate voluptuousness. In keeping with this interpretation of her appearance, the men who observe Tess read a sexual potential into her 'pouted up red mouth' (p. 450). When Alec forces a ripe strawberry between her lips, the scene is clearly proleptic of the later rape/seduction episode. When their affair ends and she leaves him, after a reluctant kiss, he comments 'You don't give me your mouth and kiss me back. You never willingly do that' (p. 111). Angel Clare too finds 'that little upward lift in the middle of her red top lip ... distracting, infatuating, maddening' as would any young man 'with the least fire in him' (p. 212). Even the narrator soon interprets her 'mobile peony mouth' as possessing eloquence. What it bespeaks is clearly her sexual attractiveness and voluptuous nature. These references culminate in the scene where Clare catches sight of her shortly after she has woken from sleep. As she yawns she reveals to him

> the red interior of her mouth as if it had been a snake's. She had stretched one arm so high above her coiled-up cable of hair that he could see its satin delicacy above the sunburn ... It was a moment when a woman's soul is more incarnate than at any other time; when the most spiritual beauty bespeaks itself flesh; and sex takes the outside place in the presentation. (pp. 242–3)

Another aspect of her physicality not usually noticed is pointed out by Dolin when he writes that 'if Tess's mouth is "consistently the most privileged feature of her appearance" her breasts are the most euphemized one' (Dolin 1998: 409). Though Hardy's wording observes the required reticence which avoided the word 'breasts' and preferred 'bosom' even for the singular form 'breast', all three men are shown to be aware of her voluptuous aspect. Alec notices it immediately and assumes her sexual accessibility. The narrator explains: 'She had an attitude which amounted to a disadvantage just now; and it was this that caused Alec d'Urberville's eyes to rivet themselves upon her. It was a luxuriance of aspect, a fullness of growth which made her appear more a woman than she really was' (p. 56). Dolin also cites a reviewer's response to this passage complaining that 'the story gains nothing by the reader being let into the secret of the physical attributes which especially fascinated him [Hardy] in Tess. Most readers can fill in the blanks for themselves without it being necessary to put the dots on the i's so very plainly' (Cox 1970: 189). Her mother, when decking her out to return to work for the d'Urbervilles, dresses her in a white frock 'the airy fullness of which ... imparted to her developing figure an amplitude which belied her age, and might cause her to be estimated as a woman when she was not much more than a child' (p. 64). Angel Clare reacts to Tess's physical appearance in the same way as Alec though, as usual, he gives a high flown gloss to the attraction he feels. Tess seemed to Clare to exhibit a dignified largeness both of disposition and physique, an almost regnant power – probably because he knew that at that time hardly any woman so well-endowed as she was likely to be walking in the open air within the boundaries of his horizon (p. 185). The handling of these features of Tess's body – which 'ought' to be invisible or non-existent – turns them instead into something to be celebrated.

Having asserted a positive value for female sexuality in a world which regards it as shameful, Hardy's text proceeds with its 'paradoxical morality' by insisting on a negative value for the very society which condemns and devalues Tess. It is ironically referred to as 'civilization'. As Hardy explained in his 1892 Preface, the readers who were unable to accept his use of the term 'pure' were stuck with the 'artificial and derivative meaning which has resulted from the ordinances of civilization'. Contemporary morality is consequently characterized as negative by its destructive effects. These primarily relate to those women who have offended against sexual *mores* though not to men who had engaged in the kind of conduct to which Clare confesses before Tess tells him of *her* past. The destructive effect of accepting such standards without qualification is illustrated not only by Clare's rejection of Tess but by the reaction even of the Marlott villagers when the Durbeyfields' lease expires. They feel that the family 'would have to go when their lease ended, if only in the interests of morality' (p. 478).

But as well as condemning 'sexual deviance' the ordinances of civilization also dictate the conduct of the vicar who, although Tess has herself baptized her dying baby cannot 'allow the plea of necessity for its irregular administration' to open the way to a Christian burial (p. 136). 'Civilization' shows no mercy to any creature human or animal. The men in a shooting party who leave wounded pheasants to die slowly in pain are said to be

> quite civil persons; save during certain weeks of autumn and winter, when, like the inhabitants of the Malay Peninsula, they ran amuck and made it their purpose to destroy life – in this case harmless feathered creatures, brought into being by artificial means solely to gratify these propensities – at once so unmannerly and so unchivalrous towards their weaker fellows in nature's teeming family. (p. 386)

It is the world of teeming nature that is apparently given a positive value in opposition to the destructive negative force of the so-called civilized social order and its morality. In the early phases of the narrative the natural world is evoked as what would flourish in a positive way if untrammelled by rigid ordinances. The narrator even ponders the question whether at some future time, the world of civilized society might change to match and merge with the more benign and positive world captured in Tess's springtime 'Rally' and her idyllic summer at Talbothays:

> In the ill-judged execution of the well-judged plan of things the call seldom produces the comer, the man to love rarely coincides with the time for loving ... We may wonder whether, at the acme and summit of the human progress these anachronisms will be corrected by a finer intuition, a closer interaction of the social machinery than that which now jolts us round and along. (p. 57)

Quite who creates the well-judged plan which the social machinery distorts is not clear. For a time the implication seems to be that it is a progressive natural world evolving towards perfection. Even Tess in the early days identifies at moments after her affair with Alex with a world of nature unconstrained by convention 'Was once lost always lost really true of chastity? she would ask herself. She might prove it false if she could veil bygones. The recuperative power which pervaded organic nature was surely not denied to maidenhood alone' (p. 140). For a time the rich natural world which restores itself cyclically figures the natural purity of Tess which, it seems, can also be restored. The image persists throughout the Talbothays episode where a benign natural world matches Tess in all her luxuriant physicality – that world where amid the 'oozing fatness and warm ferment of the Var Vale, at a season when the rush of juices could almost be heard below the hiss of fertilisation' (p. 210).

But the vision is not durable. The world of renewal fails Tess. Nature is not what it seemed. As Greenslade points out: 'In *Tess* any definition of "nature" … invites both qualification and scepticism' (Greenslade 1991: 106). The natural world proves at times as negative in its power to destroy or inflict suffering as the society which inhabits it. Already in the early part of the text, the fertility that nature bestows on human beings is seen more as a curse than a blessing. Tess, as she grew up, 'felt quite a Malthusian towards her mother for giving her so many little brothers and sisters, when it was such a trouble to nurse and provide for them' (p. 49).

Tess's son, Sorrow, brings her nothing but pain. Even at Talbothays, where nature's summer excess is matched by the sexual passion of the other milkmaids for Clare, a ludicrous misery results from their redundant natural instincts:

> The air of the sleeping chamber seemed to palpitate with the hopeless passion of the girls. They writhed feverishly under the oppressiveness of an emotion thrust on them by cruel Nature's law – an emotion which they had *neither* expected nor desired. (p. 206)

They have a 'full recognition of the futility of their infatuation, from a social point of view; its purposeless beginning; its self-bounded outlook; its lack of everything to justify its existence in the eye of civilization (while lacking nothing in the eye of Nature)' (p. 207). Teeming nature can be as ruthless in its impositions and demands as the iron rules of society. Its benign phases merely lend positive force to the naturalness and therefore the purity of Tess and provide one more source of disillusionment to afflict her.

It is relevant that there is no permanent home for Tess. After her marriage the randomly cruel aspects of the natural world to which she felt she belonged show themselves forcibly. The particularly vicious winter that afflicts Tess and her companions at Flintcomb Ash shows the indifference of nature to all its creatures. These include not only the labourers but strange birds from the north pole, 'gaunt spectral creatures with tragical eyes – eyes which had witnessed scenes of cataclysmal horror in inaccessible polar regions, of a magnitude such as no human being ever conceived, in curdling temperatures that no man could endure' (p. 397). This transformation of what had seemed at Talbothays to be a richly benign natural world echoes the comment that Hardy copied into one of his notebooks: 'Whatever we may say of nature, we cannot say that it is moral. It is often hideous, often cruel, often "red in tooth and claw"' (Bjork 1985: 2.741). The projected world of nature, in which Tess's experiences would have been no more than 'a liberal education', proves to be an illusion, a negation, a not-so, which, by contrast with Tess's unfailing altruism towards all creatures, enhances her moral stoicism.

Similarly a negative sense of self underlines her selflessness. She speaks characteristically in negative terms which show subtle changes of significance as the text progresses. Even before her 'fall' she feels shame over her sexual attractions. The men in the text, Alec, Angel and the narrator, may relish her voluptuous appearance but Tess has accepted society's standards of femininity. These decreed that, as Harry Campbell wrote in 1891, sexual instinct was 'very much less intense in women than men' (Russett 1989: 45). He believed, as did others, that in Darwinian terms such an instinct was unnecessary for women. It was therefore proper for women to be overtly sexless, as Tess is not. Consequently her sexual attractions are from the beginning something which 'had troubled her mind' (p. 56). On her way to Flintcomb Ash she disguises her beauty by wearing an old field gown and bonnet and by cutting off her eyebrows, 'resolved to run no further risks from her appearance' (p. 387). At her later meeting with the born-again Alec, there revives in her 'the wretched sentiment which had often come to her before, that in inhabiting the fleshly tabernacle with which nature

had endowed her she was somehow doing wrong' (p. 425). The rape/
seduction by Alec merely exacerbates the fallen woman's shame that
she already feels.

Her negative sense of a guilty, shameful self, then supposedly appropriate for a fallen woman, both causes and is fed by a tendency to hold
herself responsible when things go wrong for those around her. This
applies to the death of the family horse, and later the hopelessness of
the milkmaids' passion for Clare. As the narrator says of the loss of the
horse, 'Nobody blamed Tess as she blamed herself' (p. 46). With this
negative sense of her own identity embodied in a voluptuous appearance, she lacks an instinct of self-preservation. In the early stages of the
narrative she utters many refusals to comply with the requests of others
that lead ultimately to the affair with Alec. Although they are expressions of her moral instinct to avoid what seems wrong to her, her submissive actions are signs of her reluctance to make her own will and
wishes paramount. To the suggestion that she should go to Trantridge
and 'claim kin' with the d'Urbervilles, she replies uneasily 'I shouldn't
care to do that' (p. 47). It is the 'already oppressive sense of the harm
she had done' in relation to the death of the horse that leads Tess to be
'more deferential than she might otherwise have been to the maternal
wish' (p. 49). Timidly after the first visit to Trantridge, when her mother
urges her to take the work apparently offered by Alec d'Urberville's
mother, she expresses unwillingness to agree to the dubious offer and
to comply 'I don't know what to say! But – but – I don't quite like Mr.
d'Urberville being there!' (p. 62). Nonetheless she goes.

Already her dealings with Alec have alarmed her morally but guilt and
concern for her family's welfare have led her to abandon her instinctive
wish not to comply with his demands. When, in a scene proleptic of the
rape/seduction, he presses a ripe strawberry to her lips she is quick to say
'No, no!', accompanied by a deferential qualifier, 'I would rather take it
in my own hand'. But 'in slight distress she parted her lips and took it in'
(p. 55). She clearly understands the implications of his suggestive offers
and wishes to avert them. When he offers to teach her to whistle – 'I'll
give you a lesson or two' – she is quick to reply 'O no you won't!' but later
accepts (p. 80). When he attempts to kiss her, a swift 'Never!' gives way to
'Will nothing else do?' (p. 72) and compliance. Her negatives signify a
strong wish to refuse him but they are made to look like mere 'gestures' of

rejection by feelings of guilt, self-doubt and anxiety about her family.

The pattern culminates in the extreme example of the rape/seduction episode. Various alterations to the text here are relevant to the interpretation of the scene. In an early version Alec forces spirits on Tess, allegedly to keep her warm. In a later variation he gives her something from a 'druggist's bottle' which he claims is a 'cordial'. In these earlier versions there is a stronger indication that he intends rape than in the later text of 1912 where she is merely sleeping naturally. It was generally assumed that in the 1912 account, since Tess is merely asleep, Alec does not rape her. Those who took this view supported it by referring to the fact that she remains at Trantridge as his mistress for some weeks after the night in The Chase. Others who wished to argue the case for rape used as evidence the suggestion of violence in the comment of a woman working in the field where Tess feeds her baby: 'A little more than persuading had to do wi' the coming o't, I reckon. There were they that heard a sobbing one night last year in The Chase; and it mid ha' gone hard wi' a certain party if folks had come along' (p. 127).

More recently Davis makes the point that Hardy as a practising magistrate was familiar with the law relating to sexual assault. He quotes a contemporary *Digest of English Case Law*: 'to constitute rape, it is not necessary that the connection with the woman should be against her will; it is sufficient if it is without her consent' (Davis 1997: 223). Davis then describes relevant cases known to Hardy where the fact that the woman was sleeping was judicially interpreted as rendering her non-consenting and the subject of rape. Therefore he argues that what is represented in 1912 is rape followed by seduction. But presumably it follows that the inducing of sleep by spirits or drugs was also certainly rape. What is significant is the reduction in the 1912 version of strong forms of coercion.

It seems reasonable to the interpretation of the final version of the scene to assume that what is at issue in these changes is Tess's degree of participation. It is relevant to the narrator's argument that Tess's 'purity' does not depend on the sexlessness that was associated with earlier fictional attempts to defend the fallen woman. Alec, we have been told, is a practised seducer and it seems as though to Hardy the degree of economic, emotional and sexual exploitation that he exerts towards Tess means that even overt seduction would constitute rape.

Hardy does not seem to be concerned with the legalistic lines drawn to decide what constitutes rape and what does not. Alec's act is shameful, Tess's response is not. For it is made clear by her own statement to Alec that he has at some stage sexually aroused her and she has responded: 'if I had ever sincerely loved you, if I loved you still, I should not so loathe and hate myself for my weakness as I do now! ... My eyes were dazed by you for a little, and that was all' (p. 109). Later the narrator expands on this: 'She had dreaded him, winced before him, succumbed to adroit advantages he took of her helplessness; then, temporarily blinded by his ardent manners had been stirred to confused surrender awhile' (p. 117).

Offsetting Tess's feelings of worthlessness throughout these early Phases are the narrator's careful denials that her sense of guilt and shame is appropriate. On her stealthy night-time walks during her pregnancy, she feels that she is 'a figure of Guilt intruding into the haunts of Innocence'. The narrator promptly counters this:

> But all the while she was making a distinction where there was no difference. Feeling herself in antagonism she was quite in accord. She had been made to break an accepted social law, but no law known to the environment in which she fancied herself such an anomaly. (p. 121)

In the cornfield with her baby the narrator points out that Tess's misery is unnecessary and mostly generated 'by her conventional aspect, and not by her innate sensations' (p. 128). In summing up her position he is clear that, in spite of all that, her guilt and self-doubt are 'a cloud of moral hobgoblins by which she was terrified without reason. It was they that were out of harmony with the natural world not she' (p. 121).

Angel Clare proclaims himself to be similarly liberal-minded. When Tess, out of her usual guilt, tells him earnestly 'I am not worthy of you – no, I am not!' he rebukes her patronizingly:

> 'I won't have you speak like it, dear Tess! Distinction does not consist in the facile use of a contemptible set of conventions, but in being numbered amongst those who are true, and honest, and just, and pure, and lovely, and of good report – as you are, my Tess.' (p. 280)

This is ironic: as the narrator sees it those adjectives, including 'pure', all fit Tess whereas the supposedly unconventional Angel would, if he knew of her past, despise her. The consequence for Tess is that this romanticizing of her by Clare, as he interprets his own feelings flatteringly, leaves her with an increased sense of worthlessness. She articulates this early on in their relationship: 'When I see what you know, what you have read and seen and thought, I feel what a nothing I am! I'm like the poor queen of Sheba who lived in the Bible. There is no more spirit in me' (p. 179). In a desperate attempt to prevent his idealizing of her by calling her 'Artemis, Demeter and other fanciful names', she cries 'Call me Tess' (p. 186).

'Tess' for her represents the reality of the shameful self whose worthlessness becomes clearer to her as Clare presses her to marry him. Her negatives to him echo those to Alec but are more passionately vehement. She never felt unworthy of Alec but she does feel unworthy of this angel. She uttered refusals to comply with Alec's importunities because she felt them to be wrong, not with the idea of resisting temptation. To her, agreeing to marry Angel would be even more immoral because she is tempted strongly at the same time as feeling herself unworthy. Her flood of repetitively emphatic negatives focus all on the wrongness of agreeing to marry him, 'she, who could never conscientiously allow any man to marry her now' (p. 195). When the milkmaids predict that he will propose, she insists 'It cannot be' (p. 207). After he has proposed she repeats 'I cannot be your wife ... I cannot be ... I *cannot* marry you ... I don't want to marry you. I have not thought o' doing it. I cannot. I only want to love you' (p. 245). When he repeats his question she replies again 'O no, no! ... It *can't* be!' (p. 248).

Clare, who increasingly parallels Alec in his treatment of Tess, is not permanently daunted: 'His experience of women was great enough for him to be aware that a negative often meant nothing more than the preface to the affirmative' (p. 250). Like Alec, he does not recognize the true nature of her refusals: neither man can hear what she is saying. For both, her 'no' means 'yes'. Her answer to Clare the next time, however, is still the same: 'I am not worthy – not worthy enough'. He cannot read the 'hieroglyphics' which constitute the 'characters of her face' (p. 251) and sees his way as still open, even though his attempt is greeted by 'Not *again*!' (p. 254, original emphasis). Under pressure, she promises to explain to him later but only allows him a kiss. Her attempt to tell him about her past meets the same patronizing assumption that it is trivial: 'Tell it if you wish to, dearest. This precious history then. Yes: I was born at so and so, Anno Domini' (p. 270). Her courage fails and she finally agrees to marry him but does so with a sense that she is sinning: 'Yes, yes, yes! But O, I sometimes wish I had never been born' (p. 273). In the event, by using the kind of economic pressure that Alec used, Clare persuades her to fix the date of their marriage by telling her that her employer Crick will probably not need her services in the coming winter months. On their wedding day, finding herself momentarily alone, she whispers to him in her imagination 'she you love is not my real self, but one in my image; the one I might have been' (p. 304).

It is with almost these very words that he reacts when he learns of her affair with Alec on their wedding night:

> 'I repeat, the woman I have been loving is not you.'
> 'But who?'
> 'Another woman in your shape.' (p. 325)

Clare's words are more destructive to Tess than anything d'Urberville did to her. They kill her remaining sense of self. The fact that he looks upon her 'as a species of imposter, a guilty woman in the guise of an innocent one' (p. 325) confirms her own fears. His words act like those of a male Circe distorting her physically: 'her cheek was flaccid, and her mouth had almost the aspect of a round little hole' (p. 326).

Her acceptance of his judgement is total and she puts her own negatives into his mouth: 'I don't belong to you any more, then; do I, Angel?' In an ironic reversal of her marriage vows she makes a series of negative promises:

> 'I shan't ask you to let me live with you, Angel; because I have no right to. I shall not write to mother and sisters ... as I said I would ... No I shan't do anything unless you order me to. And if you go away from me, I shall not follow 'ee, and if you never speak to me any more I shall not ask you why, unless you tell me I may.' (p. 326)

Casting herself in the traditional role of a fallen woman who does not deserve to live, she ingenuously offers to act as her own executioner by drowning herself, as would be appropriate. She now believes that 'The figurative phrase was true: she was another woman than the one who had excited his desire' (p. 344). She is not the Demeter nor Artemis he superimposed on her; but then she never claimed to be.

One rebuke of Clare's that does sting Tess to an angry response is when she refers to marriages that have succeeded in spite of a woman's previous fall:

> 'Don't Tess; don't argue. Different societies, different manners. You almost make me say you are an unapprehending peasant woman, who have never been initiated into the proportions of social things. You don't know what you say.' (p. 329)

This invocation of society is in strong contrast to his fancifully egalitarian view. It echoes the usual negative view that the working classes did not take a proper attitude towards the female sexual deviance that was endemic amongst them. The class to which she belongs is now implicated in Tess's sins. Statistics seemed to support this connection, especially as a fallen woman was not distinguished from a prostitute. Many official commentaries and reports on prostitution in major cities indicated that most prostitutes came from those social groups. It was relatively easy to disregard the fact that poverty was the most frequent cause of such activity. As Walkowitz (1980) points out, the common view was that '"female fornication"' was 'symptomatic of the anomic and undisciplined nature of working-class life'. Associated with this view was a fear that the undisciplined life threatened to cause social unrest. As early as 1857 a reviewer of Acton's *Prostitution* wrote:

> It can hardly excite surprise that a sort of practical communism should prevail among the lower orders. The value of chastity is not appreciated by them as it should be … It would appear that we are 'drifting' into a sea of socialism. (Fryer 1968: 226)

Few took the view held by William Tait in his *Magdalenism* that

> the most distressing causes of prostitution are those which arise from poverty – want of employment and insufficient remuneration for needle and other kinds of work in which females are employed. (Tait 1840: 143)

When Clare says 'Different societies, different manners' he is condemning not just Tess but a whole class. The condemnation is a general one as the term 'unapprehending' makes clear. Clare's attitude widens

Hardy's project of turning negative to positive in relation to Tess alone. He had already tried to rehabilitate the agricultural worker in his article in *Longman's Magazine* (1883) on 'The Dorsetshire Labourer' (Orel 1967: 169–89) on which certain passages in *Tess* draw freely. Such labourers were, he argued, parodied by the homogenized figure of 'Hodge' as perceived by the middle and upper classes:

> a degraded being of uncouth manner and aspect, stolid understanding and snail-like movement. His speech is such a chaotic corruption of regular language that few persons of progressive aims consider it worthwhile to enquire what views, if any, of life, of nature or society are conveyed by these utterances. (Orel 1967: 168–9)

Clare has flattered himself with the belief that he now takes a more progressive view than this:

> The conventional form – folk of his imagination – personified in the newspaper press by the pitiable dummy known as Hodge – were obliterated after a few days residence. At close quarters no Hodge was to be seen.

Specifically he feels that

> The typical and unvarying Hodge ceased to exist. He had been disintegrated into a number of varied fellow creatures, beings of many minds, beings infinite in difference. (pp. 168–9)

But faced with a close example of 'female fornication' he reverts to the conventional generic view of Tess as a female Hodge, an 'unapprehending peasant woman'.

In this phrase the term 'woman' subsumes man rather then the reverse, as is usually the case. It is made clear that Tess and women like her are not, as the text presents it, the only economic victims in rural society. Tess's fate is conditioned by the poverty and, ultimately, the homelessness of her family. This in turn is linked to the wider problem of the process 'humorously described by statisticians as the "tendency of rural populations towards large towns", being really the tendency of water to flow uphill when forced by machinery' (p. 478). One of the mechanisms involved is the type of tenancy often held by families like the Durbeyfields, the account of which draws heavily on 'The Dorsetshire Labourer'. Life-holdings were a form of tenancy for the duration of named lives. When the last of these names died the tenancy ended, as the Durbeyfields' does when Tess's father dies. There were widespread and disastrous consequences:

> as the long holdings fell in they were seldom again let to simi-lar tenants, and were mostly pulled down ... Cottagers who were not directly employed on the land were looked upon with disfavour. (p. 478)

As a result it was tradesmen such as

> the carpenter, the smith, the shoemaker, the huckster and other non-descript workers ... a set of people who owed a certain stability of aim and conduct to the fact of their being life holders, like Tess's father. (p. 477)

In fact in the last thirty years of the nineteenth century 100,000 work-ers left the land in each decade.

It is not that the old-style rural life is seen as idyllic, except for the brief episode at Talbothays which points up the transience of periods of prosperity rather than their permanence. Tess, as has been pointed out, works as a *male* labourer would have done. Toiling on the land is always hard, whether it involves grubbing up swedes by hand or feeding a relentless new threshing machine. The lot of the agricultural labourer at this time was harder in general than that of the factory worker and the southern and western counties were particularly deprived. This was noticed in a government report of 1893 on 'The Agricultural Labourer'. This states that 'in these counties the large majority of labourers earn but a bare subsistence ... An immense number of them live in a chronic state of debt and anxiety, and depend to a lamentable extent upon char-ity' (Burnett 1989: 149). These are the conditions that finally leave Tess vulnerable to Alec's urgings to return to him.

Tess in her uniqueness counters belief in the stereotypical Hodge: 'beings of many minds, beings infinite in difference ... every one of whom walked in his own individual way the road to dusty death' (p. 169). She is neither the standard peasant girl over whom Alec imagines he has droit de seigneur; nor the picture-book milkmaid that Angel assumes when he thinks 'What a fresh and virginal daughter of Nature that milkmaid is' (p. 172). A denial of her iden-tity as Tess is what both men share, and for a time she fails to assert

it. A point comes however when the juxtaposition of the collapse of
the Durbeyfield family's fortunes – fatherless, homeless, penniless –
and the meeting with the newly-converted born-again Alec proves
too much. Tess is finally goaded into negatives which are denials
not of her self-worth but of what others tell her to think and do.
At first these denials are directed against Alec when she sees clearly
that his conversion is role-playing, 'less a reform than a transfigura-
tion'. She sharply denies that it is real; 'Don't go on with it ... I
can't believe in such sudden things. I feel indignant with you for
talking to me like this, when you know what harm you've done me
... Out upon such – I don't believe in you – I hate it ... such
flashes as you feel, Alec, I fear don't last' (pp. 425–6). At the same
time as refusing to see him, to marry him and his other offers, she
finally declares with conviction: 'I don't believe in anything super-
natural' (p. 438). The force of 'her negations' on the latter subject
is such as to vaporize Alec's conversion.

In overthrowing the beliefs which are theoretically the basis for the
organization of society and its ordinances, Tess finally frees herself from
a sense of worthlessness. She writes to Angel with the same directness as
she spoke to Alec:

> O why have you treated me so monstrously, Angel? I do not deserve
> it. I have thought it all over carefully, and I can never, never forgive
> you! You know that I did not intend to wrong you – why have you so
> wronged me? You are cruel, cruel indeed! I will try to forget you. It is
> all injustice that I have received at your hands! (p. 483)

Taking her fate in her own hands, she pays with her body the price
of her family's survival. Like Ida Starr she deliberately prostitutes herself. With apparent calm she poses as a married woman in a comfortable boarding house at Sandbourne in clothes suitable to Alec's rank.
Her dress was particularly offensive to reviewers. It is not the traditional gaudy finery of the kept woman but the tasteful half-mourning
of a middle-class woman who has recently lost her father. Clare's search
for her ends when he finds her 'loosely wrapped in a cashmere dressing-
gown of grey-white, embroidered in half-mourning tints ... [and] slip-
pers of the same hue' (p. 513). When she follows Clare after murdering
Alec she is in a 'walking dress' of the latest fashion and carries an ivory-
handled parasol. As Margaret Oliphant wrote indignantly 'such things

are not the accessories of purity, but the trappings of vice' (Cox 1970: 218). But Tess had abandoned such distinctions in favour of her own sense of values. In doing so she has, as Clare dimly recognizes, 'spiritually ceased to recognize the body before him as hers – allowing it to drift like a corpse upon the current, in a direction dissociated from its living will' (p. 515). She no longer sees her body as identifying her as the shameful self she believed herself to be.

She has become dangerous in overcoming the crushing impositions of civilization and their underpinning in institutionalized religion. She is in the state feared by those who saw the working classes, particularly the urbanised ones, as potential revolutionaries. As the philanthropist Stanley Smith warned in 1885: 'I am deeply convinced that the time is approaching when this seething mass of human misery will shake the social fabric, unless we grapple more earnestly with it than we have yet done ... the proletariat may strangle us' (Jones 1971: 144). It is as a woman betrayed but also as part of the 'seething mass of human misery' that Tess violently stabs Alec to death. In doing so she kills both her sexual oppressor ironically described as the son of 'an honest merchant (some said money-lender)' who made a fortune in the North and concocted a claim to the d'Urberville name (p. 51). Angel told Tess on their wedding night that since Alec was her 'husband in nature' then 'If he were dead it might be different' (p. 342). Tess, now clear in her literal-mindedness, wipes him out with the indifference and cruelty of Nature. To Angel's horror she feels no guilt. In her new state of mind and after her own bloody revolution, he finds her 'Unable to realize the gravity of her conduct, she seemed at last content; and he looked at her as she lay upon his shoulder weeping with happiness' (p. 524).

She takes control of her life and though she has few choices left and no guidelines except instinct, she seems to be empowered. Legal retribution for the murder holds no fear for her. She even makes plans for Clare's happiness after her own death by urging him to marry her younger sister, Lisa-Lu. The fact that she knows this is against the law is evident from her response to Angel's reference to the fact. Since the passing of Lord Lyndhurst's Act in 1842, one of the 'affinities' which prohibited marriage between related individuals was between a man and his dead wife's sister. Such marriages did not become legal until 1907 and were seen by some as faintly incestuous. Chambers neatly sums up the anomaly involved. She points out that 'a man and his sister-in-law were prohibited from marrying because they were considered brother and sister', but they also could not live together unmarried after the wife's death, though this might well be a convenient arrangement if there were children to be cared for 'because they were not really siblings' (Chambers 1996: 25). Tess is thus making a suggestion which in a conventional view would help to undermine the foundations of society for the sake of an individual's happiness. The blood that stains the whiteness of the ceiling below Alec and Tess's bedroom signals the horrifying chaos that the working classes can bring to their superiors.

Some of the social changes that such a revolution might bring were theoretically events that Hardy would have welcomed. He wrote in a letter that he is in favour of the break-up of 'the present pernicious conventions in respect of manners, customs, religion, illegitimacy, the stereotyped household (that it must be the unit of society), the father of a woman's child (that it is anybody's business but the woman's own)' (Purdy and Millgate 1982: 238). And Tess, true to the project of representing her as pure, surrenders herself to the inevitable death by hanging with the calm and dignity of a tragic heroine amid the timeless setting of Stonehenge, like a latter-day Iphigenia.

Hitherto the narrator, as enamoured of Tess as are Alec and Angel (or as Hardy claimed to be), has defended Tess both by denying her feelings of inadequacy and pointing up the parallel defects of Alec and Angel. But with the murder of Alec the references to her d'Urberville ancestry seem to suggest a contradictory view. This ambivalence first becomes evident at the moment of the rape when the narrator asks why such a 'coarse pattern' was destined to be imprinted on 'such beautiful feminine tissue' as Tess. He then suggests a startling possibility:

> Doubtless some of Tess d'Urberville's mailed ancestors rollicking home from a fray had dealt the same measure even more ruthlessly towards peasant girls of their time. (p. 103)

This toying with the idea that Alec's violation of Tess (significantly now for the first time referred to as d'Urberville) might be a destined retribution for the rapes perpetrated by her noble ancestors reveals that the inheritance from that ancient family is violence.

This connection between the d'Urbervilles and violence is reinforced by recurrent allusions. The tale of the d'Urberville coach is referred to by Angel; and explained to Tess by Alec when she imagines she hears the sound of a carriage and horses:

> It is that this sound of a non-existent coach can only be heard by one of d'Urberville blood, and it is held to be of ill-omen to the one who hears it. It has to do with a murder, committed by one of the family centuries ago. (p. 480)

Alec's uncertainty as to whether it was an abducted woman or a male d'Urberville who committed the murder is proleptic of his and Tess's deaths. His murder is more directly alluded to by Tess's fleeting transformation into a warrior d'Urberville when Alec speaks insultingly of Angel on the rick at Flintcomb Ash:

> One of her leather gloves … lay in her lap, and without the slightest warning she passionately swung the glove by the gauntlet directly in his face. It was heavy and thick as a warrior's, and it struck him flat on the mouth. Fancy might have regarded the act as the recrudescence of a trick in which her armed progenitors were not unpractised. (p. 452)

Later she herself makes this link with the murder; 'I feared long ago, when I struck him on the mouth with my glove, that I might do it some day for the trap he set for me in my simple youth, and the wrong to you through me' (p. 523). It is this 'ferocity' that is the very taint that Angel reads into the portraits of the d'Urberville women who resemble Tess in the house where they spend their wedding night. Clare also wonders at her remark about the glove: 'what obscure stain in the d'Urberville blood had led to this aberration if it were an aberration'. He wonders whether the story of the coach and the murder 'might have arisen because the d'Urbervilles had been known to do these things' (p. 524). Tess herself speaks of the fear of learning that she is 'just one of a long row only – finding that there is set down in some old book somebody just like me, and to know I shall only act her part' (p. 180). Her 'part' is that of the abducted woman in the d'Urberville coach and she acts it out when she stabs Alec.

Maybe it is like this, Hardy seems to be saying – maybe the cruellest joke of all in a cruel world is that Tess, in all her struggles and despite her purity of aims and will, is only able to act out a part determined by heredity. He does not commit himself to this view, any more than he commits himself to the reading of events that the narrator borrows from Aeschylus when he says that her death by hanging signals the fact that 'The President of the Immortals had ended his sport with Tess' (p. 542). He merely expresses his uncertainties and reverts, in spite of Tess, to agnosticism on issues of causality. Re-read in the light of the contradictions within the text itself, the title and subtitle of the novel might be seen not as parallels but as a disjunction: 'Tess of tainted blood and yet a pure woman'. If so, then the narrator and ultimately Hardy repeat the pattern of male betrayal for Tess already established as her last defenders desert her. What has been made of the negative value of Tess in her own society is not a positive, 'a pure woman', but a question: 'Tess – a pure woman?'.

Nobody's fault:
the structural scope of the negative
in *Little Dorrit*

'In some way negation allows us to construct new propositions out of old.' (Fogelin)

LITTLE DORRIT (1857) takes negation as its medium not only visually and verbally but structurally. Its visual framework depends on the contrast of negatives and positives. The 'Sun and Shadow' of Marseilles in the first chapter contrasts the staring whiteness in the blazing sun with the prison darkness entombing the criminals John Baptist Rigaud (alias Blandois or Lagnier) and Cavalletto (alias Altro). In the final chapter the newly married Arthur Clennam and Amy Dorrit pass along 'in sunshine and shade' (Showalter 1979). But the negatives predominate in the central locations of the Marshalsea debtors' prison and Mrs Clennam's tomb-like house. Night comes more often than day in this narrative.

In the language of a world of darkness the negative mode is the most natural form. The only manifestation of national power and government is dedicated to it and to the stasis it brings. The Circumlocution Office stands in for the whole state system:

> It is true that How not to do it was the great study and object of all public departments and professional politicians all round the Circumlocution Office. It is true that every new premier and every new government, coming in because they had upheld a certain thing as necessary to be done, were no sooner come in than they applied their utmost faculties to discovering How not to do it. It is true that from the moment when a general election was over, every returned

man who had been raving on hustings because it hadn't been done, … and who had been asserting that it must be done, … began to devise, How it was not to be done. It is true that the debates of both Houses of Parliament … uniformly tended to the protracted deliberation, How not to do it. It is true that the royal speech at the opening of such session virtually said, My lords and gentlemen, you have a considerable stroke of work to do, and you will please to retire to your respective chambers, and discuss, How not to do it. It is true that the royal speech, at the close of such session, virtually said, My lords and gentlemen, you have … been considering with great loyalty and patriotism, How not to do it, and you have found out; … All this is true, but the Circumlocution Office went beyond it. (pp. 145–6)

The effect of this negation is to seal off the governing classes from those they are supposed to govern. The separation symbolises what the historian Geoffrey Crossick calls 'the absence of a public and formal conception of the social order' in Victorian liberal ideology (Corfield 1991: 160). This refusal to see social groups as interrelated suggests an anomic society with no common set of social values and standards. Only a mixture of stasis and the resultant chaos is publicly on offer. It is the state of affairs also described by Carlyle in *Chartism* (1839) in answer to his own questions 'How an Aristocracy, in these present times and circumstances, could … set about governing the Under Class? What should they do … ?' Doing something, he declares, is 'far, very far indeed, from the "usual habits of Parliament," in late times; … had the mischief been looked into as it gradually rose, it would not have attained this magnitude. That self-cancelling Do nothingism and *Laissez-faire* should have got so ingrained into our Practice, is the source of all these miseries'. This leaves society 'full of difficulty, savagery, almost of despair' (Shelston 1986: 197–8).

The Circumlocution Office, dedicated to the maintenance of this state of affairs, depends for its existence on the negation of action: withholding/refusal/denial of information. This is illustrated repeatedly by Arthur Clennam's attempts to procure information that will allow him to clear William Dorrit's debts and release him from prison; and to establish the rights of the distinguished inventor, Daniel Doyce. But withholding communication is a disease that spreads widely to individuals outside the Office to infect society as a whole: Mrs Clennam withholds from Arthur the secret of his and her past; Miss Wade and Rigaud will not reveal the whereabouts of the stolen paper which tells the secret; Miss Wade will not disclose Harriet Beadle/Tattycoram's whereabouts when she runs away from the Meagles; Mr Casby will not tell what he knows about Miss Wade.

In other instances, communications offered are refused: ears are shut. Amy Dorrit will not listen to protestations of affection from John Chivery, son of the keeper of the Marshalsea lock. Her sister Fanny at first evades similar attention from Edmund Sparkler, stepson of the great financier Mr Merdle. Other, more elaborate resistance is practised. Miss Wade, her perceptions distorted by a sense of shame, reads all positive expressions of approval as ironic statements of negative feelings of contempt and condescension; Henry Gowan, a well connected but impoverished artist, similarly interprets any visible good in society negatively – as a sham, as not good. When, ultimately, crucial information is conveyed it is negative: Miss Wade is not legitimate; Casby is not benevolent; Merdle is not a financial genius; Mrs Clennam is *not* Arthur's mother. A textual preoccupation with negatives is easy to illustrate.

As has been shown in the previous chapter, linguistically negation is not a simple matter. It was there shown that its uses cover statements of non-existence, of rejection, of refusal to comply, and of denial. These are all semantic areas crucial to *Little Dorrit*. Each might be the figure for a central character: Amy Dorrit, Mrs General, Miss Wade, and Arthur Clennam respectively. Amy is a figure claiming non-existence; Mrs General one who rejects all that she does not wish to see; Miss Wade one who refuses to comply with what society demands of a woman; and Arthur Clennam a man who systematically denies his own feelings. But there is more to negation than this. It is complicated by the question of scope: the identification of that part of a sentence structure which is negated by the insertion of a negative form. The concept can be crudely illustrated by a comparison of two verbally similar sentences which vary as to the scope of what is negated and so differ greatly in meaning: *I do promise not to assassinate the Queen* and *I don't promise to assassinate the Queen*. The first makes a negative promise, the second makes no firm promise at all but raises a possibility. So, in handling the negative in Dickens' novelistic language, it becomes necessary to discuss not merely its detail but also its logical scope because it is architecturally structural to the narrative. The question raised by the latter is, since *Little Dorrit* is written in a negative mode, how radically is the text affected by it? How far-reaching are its negatives?

In assessing the scope of the negative in a sentence its syntax must be made clear so that the negated area can be clearly defined. The equivalent in a novel is the narrative structure/syntax. Is it linear like *Robinson Crusoe* or centrifugal like *Bleak House*? This becomes a particularly interesting question in a novel where the Circumlocution Office figures a chaotic, anomic society. The linear or picaresque structure asserts the value of a resourceful individual journeying through the obstacles society places in his way and largely evading or overcoming them. It is a structure potentially assertive of the importance of the individual over the social group as a mechanism for social order. On the other hand the centrifugal structure can naturally assert the value of the social group – in this period the family – over the individual to whom it gives identity and support. If either is outside the scope of the novel's negative force, then that structure is the affirmative meaning of the text.

Critics offer two accounts of the narrative structure of *Little Dorrit*. The first accepts the direction of the published title to take a female character as central, for the only time in a Dickens novel. The implication is that she gives coherence to the text; that she is in a sense its explanation. Though she never became what Collins calls a 'cult-figure' (Collins 1971: 357), she was seen by critics like Trilling (1955) as holding things together in a way that asserts the virtue that lies in the familial group centring on a woman, with all the ideological implications as to gender construction that this idea carries. On this reading she is a womanly figure who, like Cordelia in *King Lear*, affirms such values through the perfection of womanly silence and self (ab)negation.

The alternative account of narrative structure as linear derives from an earlier title used during the writing of the first three serial episodes – 'Nobody's Fault'. Four titles of chapters in the published work, 'Nobody's Weakness' (16), 'Nobody's Rival' (17), 'Nobody's State of Mind' (26), and 'Nobody's Disappearance' (28) identify Clennam as now (though not originally) the Nobody in question. Before he acquires this strange alternative name Arthur arrives in picaresque fashion from China to encounter whatever obstacles may face him after an absence of twenty years. He moves from group to group (his mother, the

Marshalsea prisoners, the Bleeding Heart Yarders, the Casbys, the Meagles, Henry Gowan, Mrs Merdle, Miss Wade, Cavalletto and the rest). Certainly in this obvious way he is the string onto which the beads of the narrative are threaded. His presence may be supposed to lend it coherence. A representative of those who think it does claims that 'Despite Dickens's title, it is not Little Dorrit but Arthur Clennam who occupies the novel's structural center' (Squires 1988: 50). For such critics his activity as an itinerant makes him the hero. Thus, considering the scope of the negative, the reader is faced with alternative structures; one linear with Clennam as its Tom Jones, one centrifugal with Amy as its unifying centre. So, how much of each lies within the scope of the negative?

It is the linear structure which offers itself first to the reader, despite the published title. It is Arthur who initiates the narrative on his arrival in England by revealing that he has a quest. What he is searching for is something that will link his present to his past and so confirm a positive and continuous identity essential to the functioning of the individual and so of society. This continuity is initially impossible because of his recognition that a dark secret hangs over his past. In search of a revelation he visits his mother to question her about the mystery that involves her, his dead father and himself. He finds no answer but stasis as complete as that of the Circumlocution Office: a once active woman now paralysed on 'a black, bier-like sofa' (p. 73). The paralysis figures her refusal of communication in answer to his question as to whether his father had 'unhappily wronged anyone, and made no reparation' (p. 87). Is there a negative in the past that can be made positive by atonement? Hand on bible, she denies him the facts and refuses to reopen a relationship:

> I only tell you that if you ever renew that theme with me, I will renounce you; I will so dismiss you … that you had better have been motherless from your cradle. I will never see or know you more. And if, after all, you were to come into this darkened room to look upon me lying dead, my body should bleed, if I could make it, when you came near me. (p. 90)

This leaves Arthur disconnected from his past and from her. Far from allowing reparation to repair his sense of self, she increases the burden of unfocused guilt he feels obliged to carry. She breaks the supposed continuity of the linear narrative, leaving it a brittle affair, dependent only on his moving from one group to another. In doing this he unexpectedly encounters an important figure from his past – his sweetheart Flora (now the widow Casby), from whom his mother forced him to separate twenty years earlier. Apparently, like Crusoe on his island, he has cherished a secret treasure during that time:

> In his youth he had ardently loved this woman, and had heaped upon her all the locked-up wealth of his affection and imagination. That wealth had been, in his desert home, like Robinson Crusoe's money; exchangeable with no one, lying idle in the dark to rust, until he poured it out for her. Ever since that memorable time ... he had kept the old fancy of the Past unchanged, in its old sacred place. (p. 191)

But the reality that confronts him bears so little resemblance to the past as to make him doubt whether it ever really existed. His 'lily' has not only become an overblown 'peony', but 'Flora, who had seemed enchanting in all she said and thought, was diffuse and silly' (p. 191). The sight of a fat, posturing, garrulous, middle-aged woman not only presents him with the negation of the Flora he remembers but causes him to wonder whether he misread her all along: 'Was it possible that Flora could have been such a chatterer in the days she referred to? Could there have been anything like her present disjointed volubility in the fascinations that had captivated him?' (p. 193). This meeting, like that with his mother, breaks a link and further erodes his sense of his own identity.

Turning from the past to the present, he acquires through a chance encounter on his journey home a new attachment to Minnie/Pet, the only child of the wealthy lower-middle-class couple, the Meagles. This hope for the future is however something he denies even to himself. Picaresque heroes may construct themselves positively out of the adventures they consume. Clennam completes his negative self construction with the description of what might be a new love affair. As Freud points out in his essay on 'Negation', negative statements made by certain individuals may, in areas relating to strong emotions, contain a positive assertion. It is, he asserts, a way of 'taking cognizance of what is repressed'. He tells of an 'obsessional neurotic' patient who may say:

'I've got a new obsessive idea, … and it occurred to me at once that it might mean so and so. But no; that can't be true, or it couldn't have occurred to me.' What he is repudiating … is, of course, the correct meaning of the obsessive idea.

Therefore, says Freud, 'In our interpretation, we take the liberty of disregarding the negation and of picking out the subject matter alone of the association. It is as though the patient had said: "It's true that my mother came into my mind as I thought of this person, but I don't feel inclined to let the association count"' (Strachey 1961: 235).

Clennam turns out to be a suitable case for this Freudian treatment through the period of his (non-) hopes that Pet Meagles (who eventually marries Gowan) will return his love. He watches unfolding events without taking part in them. His only action is to process the episode in his mind so as to preclude a positive outcome for himself. This is done by a skilful use of the subjunctive mood (of non-fact). Through this device his love for Pet is translated into something which might have happened but didn't. The four chapters already listed above are characterised by thoughts in which Clennam systematically denies his own feelings.

Visiting the Meagles' house his thoughts run on the lines of Freud's patient's:

Suppose that a man … who had been of age some twenty years or so … were to yield to the captivation of this charming girl, and were to persuade himself that he could hope to win her; what a weakness it would be! … Why should he be vexed or sore at heart? *It was not his weakness that he had imagined.* It was nobody's, nobody's within his knowledge; why should it trouble him? And yet it did trouble him. (p. 244)

Whereas Gowan's pursuit of Pet is accepted as present fact to be described in the indicative mood, Clennam's silent pain is always treated as the hypothetical anguish of 'Nobody's Rival':

If Clennam had not decided against falling in love with Pet; if he had had the weakness to do it; … he would have been, that night, unutterably miserable … As it was, the rain fell heavily, drearily. (p. 254)

As the courtship proceeds before his eyes, he makes no intervention, shows no resourcefulness, except in a skilful use of negatives and the subjunctive – the mood of non-fact. Using the latter he converts the present into a past in which he has already lost Pet and so describes 'Nobody's State of Mind':

> if his heart had given entertainment to that prohibited guest, his silent fighting of his way through the mental condition of this period might have been a little meritorious ... But, after the resolution he had made, of course, he could have no such merits as these; and such a state of mind was nobody's – nobody's. (pp. 356–7)

Though convinced that Gowan is a villain, he accepts the news of Pet's engagement to him without opposition and the chapter 'Nobody's Disappearance' completes his identification as Nobody: 'At that time, it seemed to him, he first finally resigned the dying hope that had flickered in nobody's heart so much to its pain and trouble' (p. 383).

Arthur, the supposed hero who links the separate groups and figures in the text, has now established a dual identity: the minimally positive one known to the world and a powerfully negative *doppelgänger*. Talking to Gowan, already discontented with Pet and her money, he shows signs of recognising this as he begins to fear that the man 'would always be a trouble to him, and that so far he had gained little or nothing from the dismissal of Nobody' – now capitalised as his proper name – 'with all his inconsistencies, anxieties, and contradictions' (p. 453). Faced with this psychological burden he decides to cut short his own story. Already in 'Nobody's State of Mind' he has become 'from that time ... in his own eyes, as to any similar hope or prospect, a very much older man who had done with that part of life' (p. 383). No more sexual love for Nobody. Since the past and present have failed him, he negates and erases the future and at forty describes himself as an old man whose life is nearly over. He elaborates on this later to Amy Dorrit when she is already the object of a love of which he has suppressed all knowledge:

> forgetting ... how old I was, and how the time for such things had gone by me with the many years of sameness and little happiness that made up my long life far away, ... forgetting all this, I fancied I loved some one ... Being wiser, I counted up my years and considered what I am, and looked back, and looked forward, ... I found that I had climbed the hill, ... and was descending quickly. (p. 432)

A feature of the picaresque hero is that he should progress by luck or resourcefulness or a capacity to survive and so provide a positive narrative dynamic. This would symbolise the ability of the individual to overcome the chaos and disconnectedness of society for himself. Clennam does the reverse of this. He subverts all progress by ruling it out in advance and resists or denies all positive impulses. He makes his own bad luck. Since he cannot progress, he circles aimlessly from group to group, trapped in his own abbreviated story. He sees himself at one stage as

> a criminal chained in a stationary boat on a deep clear river, condemned, whatever countless leagues of water flowed past him, always to see the body of the fellow-creature he had drowned lying at the bottom, immovable and unchangeable, except as the eddies made it broad or long, now expanding, now contracting its terrible lineaments. (p. 742)

Anchored by this awful burden of displaced guilt, he cannot accept that he loves Little Dorrit and so create a trajectory of desire through the narrative. He resists the knowledge that might fuel a progression until it is forced on him by John Chivery in a scene that is the apotheosis of both withholding and resisting communication. The infatuated Chivery finds it almost impossible to utter the positive statement that Amy loves Clennam, even when he wishes to comfort him for his imprisonment in the Marshalsea after the Merdle crash. Oblique hints evoke Clennam's claim not to know what he means. Chivery takes this denial as an insult to his own feelings. But Clennam only reiterates emphatically 'I don't understand it … I don't understand it … I do not understand you … I do not understand you' (p. 795–6). When the truth is uttered Clennam feels he has been dealt 'a heavy blow' (p. 797). His negative persona is damaged by the news that the woman he loves returns his love. He resists this intrusion of the positive: 'Your fancy. You are completely mistaken' (p. 797). He finds the new state of affairs 'More bewildering to him than his misery, far' (p. 798). His struggle with Nobody is painful and confused. Subjunctives only turn into questions, a halfway house to the positive:

> In the reluctance he had felt to believe that she loved any one; … in a half-formed consciousness he had had that there would be a kind

> of nobleness in his helping her love for any one, was there no sup-
> pressed something on his own side that he had hushed as it arose?
> Had he ever whispered to himself that he must not think of such a
> thing as her loving him … (p. 799)

Nobody asserts himself with the conclusion that 'Happily, if it ever
had been so, it was over' (p. 801). Any possible projection into a happy
future is thus cancelled and the present is again negatively coded with
the old skill. He has already previously cut short his own life story; he
can now merely add a full stop. Everything in 'its perspective led to her
innocent figure' and 'Looking back upon his own poor story, she was
its vanishing-point' (pp. 801–2). She is in positive terms the point at
which parallel lines in the story appear to meet, and in negative terms
the point of complete disappearance. By this doublethink he temporarily and effectively deletes her. The effectiveness derives partly from
the aptness of his description to a woman so self-effacing that her entry
into the narrative is revealed only retrospectively by Clennam's question to Affery Flintwinch: 'It was a girl, surely, whom I saw near you –
almost hidden in the dark corner?' Affery's reply confirms the willed
invisibility: 'Oh! She? Little Dorrit! *She's* nothing' (p. 80, original emphasis). In this way the linear structure is devalued by Clennam's verbal
negation of the self, which should sustain its thrust. For it is upon the
resilience of the self that the triumph of individualism over circumstance depends. The individual alone, so this structure declares, cannot
overcome the chaos of a disordered society.

The narrator, however, claims a different meaning for the self-eras-
ure that Little Dorrit shares with Tess Durbeyfield. For him it is the
essence that enables her to act as the focal point of the alternative centrifugal structure. She is supposed to hold it together and so provide a
model for the rest of society, strong and affirmative. As usual in Dickens' texts, the model is a familial group, assumed by domestic ideology
to give society coherence, order and stability. It depends on the contemporary construction of femininity. This represents 'woman's' natural qualities, when properly schooled, as creating figures like Little Dorrit
who will guard morality in general and sexual purity in particular by
perfect service at the domestic hearth. Complementary masculinity then
falls into place: self-interested, competitive and assertive. Most expo-
nents of feminine value like Florence in *Dombey and Son* or Lizzie Hexam

in *Our Mutual Friend* are marginalized. But for the narrator (and some critics), Little Dorrit is the unfolding centre of the text, not the vanishing point, despite her public self effacement. Such a view is repeatedly stressed by an unrelenting strain of narratorial approval that follows her from the age of eight. Its insistence on her feminine value and radiating beneficence seem to be what led Lionel Trilling into reading her as an overriding positive in an otherwise gloomy narrative. However, clearly he too had doubts to suppress: 'Her untinctured goodness does not appall [sic] us or make us misdoubt her as *we expect it to do*' (Trilling 1955: 65, my emphasis). If this Clennam-like suppression is avoided, the negatives in the text surface and reveal that their scope is extensive. They are both verbal and, crucially, structural.

Little Dorrit on this reading is the prime example in Dickens' work where a negative subtext reveals the contradictions which underlie both the contemporary construction of gender and the ideological representation of the family unit as an ideal. The latter ideal, if evoked as valuable, would remove the responsibility for a chaotic inequitable society from the governing classes. The negation of the idea offered by Arthur's wanderings, that individual progress is the answer to social ills, could be a preliminary to the eulogising of the family in that role. However, the eulogy itself is so dismantled as merely to provide yet further evidence of the state of affairs represented by both the Circumlocution Office and Arthur's (non) success. The dismantling is effected by the inclusion within the text's negative scope of two areas essential to the affirmation of the value of the family group: Little Dorrit's own character and her influence over others.

The central and apparently positive constituent of Little Dorrit's character, like that of other nubile girls in Dickens' novels, is disinterested kindness. This quality is identified in Sarah Stickney Ellis's contemporary conduct books for women as the one for which 'woman' is 'most valued, admired and loved'. Female examples of it in the past are identifiable because they overcame 'every impediment that intervened between them and the accomplishment of some great object', provided that it 'was wholly unconnected with their own personal exaltation or enjoyment, and related only to some beloved object whose suffering was their sorrow, whose good their gain' (Ellis 1839: 63–4).

For Dickens this is 'femininity' in its perfect form and Little Dorrit embodies it. Femaleness was something different: a biologically determined set of characteristics of a non-intellectual, intuitive, reactive kind. Unchecked, these produced unreasonable, emotional, demanding and often insanely garrulous monsters like Mrs Nickleby, Mrs Skewton, Mrs Joe Gargery, Mrs Wilfer, and others (Ingham, 1992). The magic ingredient that turns the female into the feminine is the very one that Little Dorrit has in abundance: plasticity when faced with the needs of others. Upon this the creation of feminine value depends. That is why Little Dorrit is to be so highly valued: because she is able to transmit her power from the centre to others, in the form of long-sufferingness, compassion and affection. She is supposedly able to do this because she stands in a parental role to those around her. It is significant that for Dickens a 'true' woman, as opposed to a female in her natural state, is necessarily 'a mother'. Not in a biological sense for such people either by typical carelessness die prematurely or, lacking plasticity, turn to self nurturing like Mrs Clennam. 'True' motherhood is most frequently found in innocently nubile girls who achieve it in a surrogate fashion which also turns them into virginal wives. In the nineteenth century the frequency of maternal death in or soon after childbirth often led to a daughter or a wife's sister taking on the chief domestic burden of a family. As Davidoff and Hall (1987) point out, strong bonds frequently grew up between widower and housekeeper. She became a kind of substitute mother and partner. Hence the necessity, given the incest taboo, for a prohibition on marriage with a deceased wife's sister, alluded to in *Tess*, which persisted until 1907.

This is, in practical terms, the kind of role that Little Dorrit moves into after the early death of her mother. Narratorial eulogy wraps it round with a particular air of sanctity. Her ability to nurture is supposedly demonstrated by arranging, under great difficulties, for her sister Fanny to train as a dancer, and by finding her brother Tip/Edward a string of jobs to lose and a chance of emigration to throw away. Most of all, the satisfaction of her father's needs is figured as religious:

> She filled his glass, put all the little matters on the table ready to his hand, and then sat beside him while he ate his supper. Evidently in observance of their nightly custom, she put some bread before herself, and touched his glass with her lips. (p. 122)

Her domestic services take on a sacramental tone that in a mid-Victorian text is faintly blasphemous in giving her even a minor priestly role.

However, Little Dorrit – like Clennam – has an alternative persona and, like his, it functions through verbal negation. In this guise she may be conveniently referred to as Amy. As Little Dorrit she possesses, for instance in the Clennam house, what some regard as a Cordelia-style capacity for womanly silence. As the secret Amy she shows herself a perfect liar – often by *not* speaking. Even her skill in meeting her father's domestic needs is surpassed by her skill in pandering to his obsessions. Thanks to her, he is able to sustain even in the debtors' prison a fantasy that he has a special dignity and social standing, and a special respect and affection from those around him. Silence is here her chief tool. She does *not* tell him the truth about his son's distressing profligacy, nor her own grinding work as a seamstress, nor Fanny's as a dancer. She conceals the fact that the devoted brother Frederick, whom he has absent-mindedly ruined, is earning a meagre living in a shabby theatre orchestra. As Godmother of the Dorrit Mafia she manipulates all those involved into colluding with the code of silence. With his fantasy secure, Dorrit can also be prevented from knowing that his moderate comfort is achieved at the expense of others. He can wound well-meaning onlookers like Chivery and Old Nandy without paying any penalty. Little Dorrit's capacity in this particular area of concealment, denial and lying by silence makes the genteel Mrs General's skill in mere 'varnishing' look amateurish. All the latter does, to much derision from the narrator, is to 'varnish':

> Mrs General was not to be told of anything shocking. Accidents, miseries, and offences, were never to be mentioned before her. Passion was to go to sleep in the presence of Mrs General, and blood was to change to milk and water. The little that was left in the world, when all these deductions were made, it was Mrs General's province to varnish … she dipped the smallest of brushes into the largest of pots, and varnished the surface of every object that came under consideration. The more cracked it was, the more Mrs General varnished it. (p. 503)

Amy goes beyond this to deny the existence of realities altogether. Further, there are indications that Amy's disinterested kindness is not so disinterested after all. The subservient relationship to her father takes on a new implication when on three occasions she displays sexual jealousy towards him. These occur when the question of a sexual partner for one or other of them occurs. In the first, she is mildly harassed by the attentions of John Chivery who has become infatuated with her. She regards her father's encouragement of him, and hints to her to string him along, as little less than pimping. Her 'O dear, dear Father, how can you, can you, do it!' (p. 261) is more suited to a wife than an unmarried daughter. Similarly she responds inappropriately to the lover's kiss that Clennam gives her after the news that her father is to be free and inherit a fortune. She reacts as though he were her father: 'As he kissed her, she turned her head towards his shoulder, and raised her arm towards his neck; cried out "Father! Father! Father!" and swooned away' (p. 465).

A later episode makes it plain that Amy will brook no rival for her father's affections when he becomes enamoured of his daughters' companion. Fanny Sparkler (née Dorrit) is against a match with Mrs General on financial grounds but Amy refuses to recognise what is happening. The truth is forced on her only by her father's suggestion that she should do as Fanny did:

> 'Amy ... your dear sister, our Fanny, has contracted – ha hum – a marriage, eminently calculated to extend the basis of our – ha – connection, and to – hum – consolidate our social relations. My love, I trust that the time is not far distant when some – ha – eligible partner may be found for you'. (p. 669)

The expression of her repugnance to her father's marriage is characteristically minimal but its motive is very different from Fanny's. It springs from a jealous sense of betrayal, cast in the hypothetical subjunctive mood that Clennam favours, and denied (like Clennam's love) even as it dawns:

> If the thought ever entered Little Dorrit's head that night, that he could give her up lightly now in his prosperity, and when he had it in his mind to replace her with a second wife, she drove it away. Faithful to him still, ... she drove the thought away. (p. 670)

There is a literal truth in the idea that Mrs General would be William Dorrit's second wife, replacing Amy's mother; but the girl's own phrase 'replace her' referring to herself makes *her* the faithful wife who is to be displaced. The insistence on driving out, even the thought of another wife, indicates a picture too horrible to contemplate of herself supplanted, betrayed, in effect divorced.

Sadoff argues away the incestuously sexual overtones of these scenes. She reads William Dorrit as a mere surrogate from whom in due course love is transferred to the 'real' lover, Arthur Clennam:

> When I use the term 'incestuous' with regard to Dickens' fathers and daughters, I mean they create a community built on familial structures of desire yet also purified of desire and perfected through idealized love. The figure of the daughter draws to herself the father and the lover – the father as lover, the lover as father – and also redeems the desire that calls this incestuous structure into being. (Sadoff 1982: 55)

This is all very well as an abstract argument but is vitiated by the fact that, by contrast with Amy's jealousy of her father, her relationship with Clennam in the text remains sexless on both sides.

He always thinks of her as 'Little Dorrit' not Amy, his 'delicate child', his 'adopted child'. After Chivery's revelation that she loves him he has to try in his 'stunned' state, to transform her in his mind into a normal adult woman: 'He had been accustomed to call her his child, and his dear child, and to invite her confidence by dwelling upon the difference in their respective ages, and to speak of himself as one who was turning old. Yet she might not have thought him old' (p. 798). His struggle is to free himself from an ingrained practice of denial and from any sense that sexual love for her would be paedophiliac. Her response to him involves an easier transition to the role of mother. When they become recognised lovers while he is imprisoned in the Marshalsea, 'drawing an arm softly round his neck, [she] laid his head upon her bosom, put a hand upon his head, and resting her cheek upon that hand, nursed him as lovingly, and GOD knows as innocently, as she had nursed her father in that room when she had been but a baby, needing all the care from others that she took of them' (p. 825). She *has* grown into an adult woman but simultaneously turned into the mother he has never had, not a sexual partner. Her image of him has long been visually negative and non-sexual: 'the shadow' whom, in her tale to Maggie, the 'tiny woman' treasures in a secret place until she dies and it disappears (pp. 339–43).

Her long nursing of her father, on the other hand, is figured as less 'innocent' than this. Its eroticism is irrevocably crystallised in the image of Amy as 'The Roman Charity'. This was a familiar icon in pictorial art from the Renaissance onwards and frequent in the Victorian period. Its most cited classical source is evidently Valerius Maximus (Meisel 1983: 305). It appears when William Dorrit throws a fit of histrionic self-pity to evade the consequences of his mean part in the Chivery affair. His daughter responds heroically:

> There was a classical daughter once – perhaps – who ministered to her father in his prison as her mother had ministered to her. Little Dorrit, though of the unheroic modern stock and mere English, did much more, in comforting her father's wasted heart upon her innocent breast, and turning it to a fountain of love and fidelity that never ran dry or waned through all his years of famine. (pp. 273–4)

What Amy offers her father is endless mother's milk, in the apotheosis of her nurturing function. The circumlocutory nature of the reference to breastfeeding, the appeal to the respectability of classical authority, and the hypothesizing inference of 'perhaps' cannot take away from the shock of a young female endlessly suckling an adult male.

The eroticism of such an action is evident from the pictorial versions of the scene. The disturbing effect in the novel is increased by the dual identity of the woman. Amy is woman enough to suckle a man but Little Dorrit is 'a child'. Her pre-pubertal appearance is implicit in her nickname which has been so insisted upon, even by Clennam. She is 'little' or slight in appearance/asexual-looking: 'A woman, probably of not less than two-and-twenty, she might have been passed in the street for little more than half that age' (p. 93). This early description has been constantly kept in mind by her name and pinned to the masthead of the novel as its title. It has been underlined also by the contrast with the overgrown and retarded woman Maggie, child in mind but woman in body. There is a moment when the text registers an unexpected awareness that what the narrator is offering as the stable centre of the centrifugal structure, an example of the womanly ideal perfectly achieved, is monstrous in her duality. This is when a prostitute, who has mistaken Amy for a child out too late at night and Maggie for her careless nurse, realises her mistake as she kisses 'the child's' cheek: 'Why, my God!' she said, recoiling, 'you're a woman!' (p. 218). This horrified reaction to a child-woman is structurally negated and dissociated from by being put into the mouth of a non-person, a prostitute. But the gratuitousness of the episode, which has no bearing on any event in the novel, enforces a reading of the passage as emphatic: a Little Dorrit/ Amy, a child-woman, is a manifest horror. This is compounded only further by the canonization of the child-woman as the Roman Charity. No eulogy from the narrator can disguise the doubly incestuous nature of the scene in which the female figure is indistinguishably daughter, mother and lover.

These confusions rather than a sense of social order and fulfilment for individuals speak out through the centrifugal structuring of the text. Consequently the proper roles of the other members of the Dorrit family are unclear to them. Tip and Fanny, in relation to Amy, oscillate between submissiveness towards a parent and resentment towards a younger sister. Tip becomes overdependent on the maternal figure of Amy; Fanny strikes out to find an independent identity for herself in another family group by marrying the rich idiot, Edmund Sparkler. There is no positive outcome for either: Tip deteriorates into a moral/ physical illness through which his younger sister nurses him to an early death; Fanny finds that, after the Merdle crash, her rich idiot is no longer rich. The wealth and social position, which were dependent on it, have disappeared. She must live forever, bosom by bosom, with Sparkler's hated mother, Mrs Merdle, and 'fight it out in the lists of Society, sworn rivals' (p. 874). Total destruction, however, is the lot of the father/child husband in whom Amy has invested most of her nurturing milk. Thanks to her careful protection of his fantasies which transformed his prison life into a kingdom, William Dorrit cannot deal with the reality of life even in the shape of untold wealth and social prestige. With her help, he accommodated to prison life, but he cannot accommodate to the real world. His public breakdown at a Roman banquet is a retreat into the old comfortable fantasy as Father of the Marshalsea. Amy too has accommodated herself to the domestic life in prison with her father. She takes no pleasure in the sights of Italy and speaks of a terrible 'home-sickness' (p. 610), presumably for the only home she has ever known, the debtors' prison. The ruins of Rome are for her 'ruins of the old Marshalsea – ruins of her own old life … ruins of its loves, hopes, cares, and joys' (p. 671). When her father's delusion scatters the Roman dinner party, she returns with relief to that narrow and crippling past. Its destructive nature is evident as it kills both William Dorrit and that other dependent child of hers, his brother Frederick. Yet she is at ease with herself as grieving mother in a way that she never was as a jealous partner to a rich man.

Thus Little Dorrit/Amy herself is ultimately a contradictory and disruptive figure who sustains nothing more than a sadly dysfunctional family. The narrator, however, drives away the thought, as Amy did, and insists on a conventionally eulogistic reading of her. Like the linear structure, the centrifugal one based on the family group as a model of social harmony is negated, not merely verbally but structurally through the workings of the plot. Consequently the scope of the negative in *Little Dorrit* is comprehensive: both solutions to a society without order or common values are put under the sign of negation. No reading of society can be found that offers hope for its reform. Only the chaos remains, as the pictorial summation of the novel on the cover of the serial number of the text shows. This presents a jumbled procession of characters shambling in a pointless and disorderly circle. *Little Dorrit*, far from offering a picture of the family as a harmonious and benign unit on which society can model itself, reveals it despite narratorial approval as manipulative and destructive.

The counterview to conventional domestic ideology was expressed by a few individual voices even in the mid-nineteenth century. One was that of Florence Nightingale in a work written in 1852 that only appeared as an interlude in a religious volume privately printed in 1860. In it she says outrageously:

> The family? It is too narrow a field for the development of an immortal spirit … The family uses people, *not* for what they are, not for what they are intended to be, but for what it wants them for – for its own uses … This system dooms some minds to incurable infancy, others to silent misery. (Stark 1979: 37, original emphasis)

In Dickens' text the conventional view and the outrageous are in conflict. It is only under the safety of negation that the contradictions inherent in the contemporary construction of gender are exposed. This is the first step in a popular mainstream writer towards a recognition of what ideology suppresses. The image of the Circumlocution Office makes a strong assertion that a society consisting of governors and underclass is necessarily anomic. The only alternatives offered by the text as possible counters to this view, individualism or family groupings, are invalidated by the negative form in which they appear. This invalidation is of course covert and surreptitious. As Freud says in his essay on 'Negation', 'the function of judgement is not made possible until the creation of the symbol of negation has endowed thinking with a first measure of freedom from the consequences of repression' (Strachey 1961: 239). In the language of *Little Dorrit* negation releases underlying contradictions in the construction of gender and social class that offer some such freedom of expression. It is a striking example of how the 'invisible' mechanisms of language contribute to the fluidity of ideologies of language in an unobtrusive but radical way.

Postscript

THE topics discussed in the individual chapters above may appear random. In fact, though not exclusive of others, they constitute a coherent whole in terms of the nature of narrative.

Since narrations are linear and sequential, they necessarily involve the handling of time and place of what is described in relation to the supposed narrator. The same is true of any utterance. But the necessary use of tense does not simply relate to the timing of events: it has a role in indicating the attitude of the narrator to what he or she recounts. Such narrators were formerly referred to as 'reliable' or 'unreliable' in their approach. In practice, as has been shown, their perspective on what is related often fluctuates between varying degrees of certainty and doubt, or in linguistic terms 'modality'. Also contributing to modality, or attitude to the truth or rightness of the narrative is the use of questions. These obviously raise doubts about aspects of plot or motive. Negations can work in the same way to problematize the perspective on events and characters.

It was claimed in chapter 1 that these aspects of language were usually invisible to the reader. Successive chapters attempted to make them visible and to analyze their role in the significance of the text. When this is done there is a partial revelation of how language and ideology connect. In the many varying accounts of ideology one consistently observed feature is that it works to make normal or natural certain assumptions about the society we live in. These assumptions are usually unnoticed on a day-to-day basis, though they inhabit the language we use. What a sharp focus on such linguistic features as the functioning of tense, deixis, questions and negations can do is denaturalize these assumptions and bring them to light. In making language visible we can do the same for ideology and its contradictions.

References

Altick, R. (ed.) (1977) *Thomas Carlyle, Past and Present*, New York: New York University Press.

Baker, H. A. (ed.) (1986) *Narrative of the Life of Frederick Douglass, An American Slave*, Harmondsworth: Penguin.

Barrett, M. (1988) *Women's Oppression Today*, New York: Verso.

Barthes, R. (1970) *S.Z.*, Paris: Seuil.

Beer, G. (ed.) (1996) *Charles Darwin: The Origin of Species*, Oxford: Oxford University Press.

Bignell, J. (1997) *Media Semiotics*, Manchester: Manchester University Press.

Björk, L. A. (ed.) (1985) *The Literary Notebooks of Thomas Hardy*, London and Basingstoke: Macmillan Press, 2 parts (3 vols): part I (2 vols) and part II (1 vol.).

Blount, T. (ed.) (1996) *Charles Dickens, David Copperfield*, Harmondsworth: Penguin.

Bostock, S. (ed.) (1987) *Feminist Issues in Literary Scholarship*, Bloomington: Indiana University Press.

Bradbury, N. (ed.) (1996) *Charles Dickens, Bleak House*, Harmondsworth: Penguin.

Burnett, J. (1989) *Plenty and Want: A Social History of Food in England from 1815 to the Present Day*, London: Routledge.

Butt, J. and Tillotson, K. (1968) *Dickens at Work*, London: Methuen and Co.

Byatt, A. S. and Warren, N. (eds) (1990) *George Eliot, Selected Essays, Poems and Other Writings*, Harmondsworth: Penguin.

Carey, J. (ed.) (1981) *James Hogg, The Private Memoirs and Confessions of a Justified Sinner*, Oxford: Oxford University Press.

Carroll, D., (ed.) (1971) *George Eliot: The Critical Heritage*, London: Routledge and Kegan Paul.

Chambers, D. M. (1996) 'Triangular Desire and the Sororal Bond: The "Deceased Wife's Sister Bill"', *Mosaic* 29: 19–36.

Cheyette, B. (1993) *Constructions of 'the Jew' in English Literature and Society: Racial Representations, 1875–1945*, Cambridge: Cambridge University Press.

Chomsky, N. (1965) *Aspects of Syntax*, Cambridge, Mass: MIT Press.

Clark, K. (ed.) (1964) *John Ruskin, Selected Writings*, Harmondsworth: Penguin.

Cockshut, A. O. J. (ed.) (1994) *John Ruskin, Praeterita*, Keele: Ryburn Publishing, Keele University Press.

Collins, P. (ed.) (1971) *Dickens: The Critical Heritage*, New York: Barnes and Noble.

Connor, S. (ed.) (1996) *Charles Dickens* (Longman Critical Reader), London and New York: Longman.

Corfield, P. J. (ed.) (1991) *Language, History and Class*, Oxford: Basil Blackwell.

Cox, R. G. (ed.) (1970) *Thomas Hardy: The Critical Heritage*, New York: Barnes and Noble.

Culler, J. (1975) *Structualist Poetics: Structualism, Linguistics, and the Study of Literature*, London: Routledge and Kegan Paul.

Davidoff, L. and Hall, C. (eds) (1987) *Family Fortunes: Men and Women of the English Middle Class 1780–1850*, London: Hutchinson.

Davis, W. A. Jr. (1997) 'The Rape of Tess: Hardy, English Law, and the Case for Sexual Assault', *Nineteenth-Century Literature*, 23: 221–31.

de Beer, G. (ed.) (1974) *Charles Darwin and Thomas Henry Huxley, Autobiographies*, London: Oxford University Press.

Dolin, T. and Higonnet, M. (eds) (1998) *Thomas Hardy, Tess of the D'Urbervilles*, Harmondsworth: Penguin.

Dowling, L. (1982) 'Victorian Oxford and the Science of Language', *PMLA* 97: 160–78.

Ellis, S. S. (1839) *The Women of England, Their Social Duties and Domestic Habits*, London: Fisher.

Ellis, S. S. (1843a) *The Wives of England: Their Relative Duties, Domestic*

Influence and Social Obligations, London: Fisher.

Ellis, S. S. (1843b) *The Mothers of England: Their Influence and Responsibilities*, London: Fisher.

Fielding, K. J. (ed.) (1960) *The Speeches of Charles Dickens*, Oxford: Clarendon Press.

Ford, G. and Monod, S. (eds) (1966) *Charles Dickens, Hard Times*, New York: W. W. Norton and Co.

Frow, J. (1986) *Marxism and Literary History*, Oxford: Basil Blackwell.

Fryer, P. (ed.) (1968) *William Acton, Prostitution*, New York and Washington: Frederick A. Praeger.

Greenslade, W. (1991) 'The Lure of Pedigree in *Tess of the D'Urbervilles*', *Thomas Hardy Journal* 7(3): 103–115.

Grindle, J. and Gatrell, S. (eds) (1983) *Thomas Hardy, Tess of the d'Urbervilles*, Oxford: Clarendon Press.

Haight, G. S. (ed.) (1954–78) *The George Eliot Letters*, Oxford: Oxford University Press, 9 vols.

Haight, G. S. (ed.) (1980) *George Eliot, The Mill on the Floss*, Oxford: Clarendon Press.

Haight, G. S. (ed.) (1984) *George Eliot, Daniel Deronda*, Oxford, Clarendon Press.

Harris, R. (trans.) (1983) *Ferdinand de Saussure, Course in General Linguistics*, London: Duckworth.

Hawkes, J. (trans.) (1982) *The London Journal of Flora Tristan: The Aristocracy and the Working Class of England*, London: Virago.

Heller, D. and Cohen, D. (eds) (1990) *Jewish Presence in English Literature*, Montreal and Kingston: McGill Queens University Press, pp. 76–95.

Helsinger, E. K., Sheets, R. L. and Veeder, W. (eds) (1983) *The Woman Question: Social Issues 1837–1883*, 3 vols., Manchester: Manchester University Press.

Hirsch, P. (1994) 'Women and Jews in *Daniel Deronda*', *George Eliot Review* 25: 45–50.

Holquist, M. (ed.) (1981) *The Dialogic Imagination, Four Essays by M. M. Bakhtin*, Austin: University of Texas Press.

Ingham, P. (1992) *Dickens, Women and Language*, Hemel Hempstead: Harvester Wheatsheaf.

Jewsbury, G. (1848) *The Half Sisters*, London: Chapman and Hall.

Jewsbury, G. (1851) *Marion Withers*, London: Colburn and Co.

Jones, G. S. (1971) *Outcast London: A Study in the Relationship between*

Classes in Victorian Society, Oxford: Clarendon Press.

Kaufmann, D. (1977) *George Eliot and Judaism: An Attempt to Appreciate 'Daniel Deronda'*, Edinburgh and London: William Blackwood & Sons.

Kranidis, R. S. (ed.) (1998) *Imperial Objects: Victorian Women's Emigration and the Unauthorized Imperial Experience*, London: Prentice Hall International.

Le Quesne, A. L., Landow, G. P., Collini, S., and Stansky, P. (eds) (1993) *Victorian Thinkers*, Oxford: Oxford University Press.

Linehan, K. B. (1992) 'Mixed Politics: The Critique of Imperialism in *Daniel Deronda*', *Texas Studies in Literature and Language*, 34(3): 323–46.

Lipman, S. (ed.) (1994) *Matthew Arnold, Culture and Anarchy*, New Haven and London: Yale University Press.

Lyons, J. (1978) *Semantics*, 2 vols., Cambridge: Cambridge University Press.

Mandel, E. and Fowkes, B (eds) (1990) *Karl Marx, Capital*, vol. 1, Harmondsworth: Penguin.

Martin, C. A. (1988) 'Contemporary Critics and Judaism in *Daniel Deronda*', *Victorian Periodicals Review* 21(3): 90–107.

Mason, M. (ed.) (1996) *Charlotte Brontë, Jane Eyre*, Harmondsworth: Penguin.

Matejka, L. and Titunik, R. (trans.) (1986) *V. V. Volosinov, Marxism and the Philosophy of Language*, Cambridge, Mass., and London: Harvard University Press.

Meisel, M. (1983) *Realizations: Pictorial and Theatrical Arts in Nineteenth-Century England*, Princeton: Princeton University Press.

Meyer, S. (1993) 'Safely to their Own Borders: Proto-Zionism, Feminism, Nationalism in *Daniel Deronda*', *ELH* 60(3): 733–58.

Miller, A. (1990) '*Vanity Fair* through Plate Glass', *PMLA* 105(5): 1042–54.

Miller, A. (1995) *Novels Behind Glass: Commodity Culture and Victorian Narrative*, Cambridge: Cambridge University Press.

Miller, N. K. (1988) *Subject to Change: Reading Feminist Writing*, New York: Columbia University Press.

Nead, L. (1988) *Myths of Sexuality: Representations of Women in Victorian Fiction*, Oxford: Basil Blackwell.

Norton, S. M. (1993) 'The Ex-Collector of Boggley Wollah: Colonialism in the Empire of *Vanity Fair*', *Narrative* 1(2): 124–37.

Orel, H. (ed.) (1967) *Thomas Hardy's Personal Writings*, London and Melbourne: Macmillan.

Purdy, R. L., and Millgate, M. (eds) (1979) *The Collected Letters of Thomas Hardy 1840–1892*, vol. 1, Oxford: Clarendon Press.

Purdy, R. L., and Millgate, M. (eds) (1982) *The Collected Letters of Thomas Hardy 1902–1908*, vol. 3, Oxford: Clarendon Press.

Quiller-Couch, A. (1943) (ed.) *The Oxford Book of English Verse*, Oxford: Clarendon Press.

Ray, G. N. (ed.) (1945–46) *The Letters and Private Papers of William Makepeace Thackeray*, London: Oxford University Press.

Rignall, J. (1993) 'Metaphor, Truth and the Mobile Imagination in *The Mill on the Floss*', *George Eliot Review* 24: 36–40.

Roe, S. (ed.) (1987) *Women Reading Women's Writing*, Brighton: Harvester Press.

Ruskin, J. (1903) *Unto this Last: Four Essays on the First Principles of Political Economy*, London: George Allen.

Russett, C. E. (1989) *Sexual Science: The Victorian Construction of Womanhood*, Cambridge, Mass., and London: Harvard University Press.

Sadoff, D. (1982) *Monsters of Affection: Dickens, Eliot and Brontë on Fatherhood*, Baltimore and London: Johns Hopkins University Press.

Secord, J. A. (ed.) (1997) *Charles Lyell, Principles of Geology*, Harmondsworth: Penguin.

Shelston, A. (ed.) (1986) *Thomas Carlyle: Selected Writings*, Harmondsworth: Penguin.

Shillingsburg, P. (1993) 'Watching Thackeray Decide Who Says and Who Knows What in *Vanity Fair*', *Thackeray Newsletter* 37: 11.

Showalter, E. (1979) 'Guilt, Authority and the Shadows of *Little Dorrit*', *Nineteenth-Century Fiction* 34: 20–40.

Shuttleworth, S. (1996) *Charlotte Brontë and Victorian Psychology*, Cambridge: Cambridge University Press.

Smith, J. (1991) '"The Wonderful Geological Story": Uniformitarianism and *The Mill on the Floss*', *Papers on Language and Literature* 27(4): 430–52.

Smith, S. M. (1980) *The Other Nation: The Poor in the English Novels of the 1840s and 1850s*, Oxford: Clarendon Press.

Squires, M. (1988) 'The Structure of Dickens's Imagination in *Little Dorrit*', *Texas Studies in Literature and Language* 30: 49–64.

Stallybrass, O. (ed.) (1985) *E. M. Forster, A Passage to India*, Oxford: Oxford University Press.

Stark, M. (ed.) (1979) *Florence Nightingale, Cassandra*, New York: Feminist Press, University of New York.

Strachey, J. (ed.) (1961) *The Standard Edition of the Complete Psychological Works of Sigmund Freud* 19: 235–9, London: Hogarth Press.

Sussman, H. (1995) *Masculinities: Manhood and Masculine Poetry in Early Victorian Literature and Art*, Cambridge: Cambridge University Press.

Sutherland, J. (ed.) (1998) *William Makepeace Thackeray, Vanity Fair*, Oxford: Oxford University Press.

Tait, W. (1840) *Magdalenism: An Inquiry into the Extent, Causes and Consequences of Prostitution*, Edinburgh.

Thomas, D. (1992) 'Miss Swartz and the Hottentot Venus Revisited', *Thackeray Newsletter*, 36: 1–5.

Tillotson, G. and Hawes, D. (eds) (1968) *Thackeray: the Critical Heritage*, London: Routledge and Kegan Paul.

Traugott, E. C. and Pratt, M. L. (1980) *Linguistics for Students of Literature*, New York: Harcourt Brace Jovanovich.

Trilling, L. (1955) *The Opposing Self: Nine Essays in Criticism*, London: Secker and Warburg.

Trodd, A. (ed.) (1998) *Wilkie Collins, The Moonstone*, Oxford: Oxford University Press.

Walker, A. (1834) *Physiognomy Founded on Physiology and Applied to Various Countries, Professions and Individuals*, London: Smith Elder.

Walkowitz, J. (1980) *Prostitution and Victorian Society: Women, Class and the State*, Cambridge: Cambridge University Press.

Wall, S. (ed.) (1998) *Charles Dickens, Little Dorrit*, Harmondsworth: Penguin.

Widdowson, P. (ed.) (1982) *Re-Reading English*, London and New York: Methuen, pp. 121–35.

Wing, B. (trans.) (1986) *The Newly Born Woman*, Manchester: Manchester University Press.

Yates, G. G. (ed.) (1985) *Harriet Martineau on Women*, New Brunswick, N.J.: Rutgers University Press.

Index

adaptation 105
American Civil War 71–2
Amoretti (Spenser) 123
Arnold, Matthew 41, 80
asking questions 16–17
Auden, W. H. 96

Bakhtin, M. M. 6–8
Barnaby Rudge (Dickens) 40
Barrett, Michele 6
Barthes, Roland 5
Bildungsroman 45, 94
Bleak House (Dickens) 9, 10, 43
   desire 104–5
   identity 99–103
   narrative structure 147
   narrators 93, 96–9, 106–11,
     114–15
   social classes 110–14
   social distortion 105–6
   tense 39–40
Bopp, Franz 42
Boumelha, Penny 62
Brontë, Charlotte

Jane Eyre 99, 101
Shirley 23, 101, 110
Villette 103

Campbell, Harry 130
Carlyle, Thomas
   do-nothingism 114, 145
   social class 21–3, 27–9
   time 39, 40, 47
Carroll, D. 57, 58, 59
Cassandra (Nightingale) 101, 103,
   105
centrifugal narrative structure 147,
   160–1
Chambers, D. M. 140–1
Cheyette, Bryan 63, 77, 80
childhood 40–1, 48–50
Chomsky, N. 4
chronotopes 7–8
civilization 127–8, 140
Cixous, H. 21
code-switching 5
codes 3, 4, 5
Cohen, D. 78

Collins, P. 147
Collins, Wilkie 97–8, 99
commodification
    Daniel Deronda 79, 81
    Vanity Fair 33–6
communicative competence 4–5
competence 4
Coningsby (Disraeli) 113
Crossick, Geoffrey 29, 145
Culler, Jonathan 4–5

Daniel Deronda (Eliot) 9
    contemporary events 71–3
    death 83–4
    femininity 79–80
    future 63, 65, 67, 70, 73–4, 78
    gain and loss 81–2, 89
    identity 67–9
    imperialism 74–6, 88
    Judaism 76–8, 80–1
    magic future 85–7
    past 69–70, 71
    women 79
Darwin, Charles
    childhood 40
    habitual reference 96, 109
    natural history 42, 43, 45
    relatedness 47, 110
David Copperfield (Dickens) 94
Davidoff, L. 155
Davis, W. A. Jr. 132
death 35–6, 83–4
deixis 8–9, 94
denial 121, 139, 146, 150
desire 82–3, 104–5, 106
Dickens, Charles
    Barnaby Rudge 40
    Bleak House 93–4, 96–117
    David Copperfield 94
    Dombey and Son 153
    Hard Times 34

Little Dorrit 104, 114, 144–64
Our Mutual Friend 153–4
sanitation 111–12
A Tale of Two Cities 40
discourse 4
Disraeli, Benjamin 111, 113
Dolin, T. 126–7
domain *see* scope
Dombey and Son (Dickens) 153
Douglass, Frederick 81, 82, 84

Eliot, George
    Daniel Deronda 63, 67–89
    Middlemarch 71, 84
    The Mill on the Floss 39, 40, 42,
        43–62, 63
    'The Natural History of
        German Life' 45, 46, 56
Eliot, T. S. 16–18
Ellis, Sarah Stickney 22, 29, 154
emigration 88–9
emphasis 122
epistemic modality 9

femininity
    Daniel Deronda 79–80
    Little Dorrit 153–5
    The Mill on the Floss 57–8, 60
    Vanity Fair 23–6, 27
Forster, E. M. 95
Forster, John 26
Free Indirect Speech (FIS) 7
Freud, Sigmund 149–50, 162
Frow, J. 3–4
future 64–7
    Daniel Deronda 63, 70, 73–4,
        78

gain and loss, *Daniel Deronda* 81–
    2, 89
Gaskell, Elizabeth 23, 110, 125–6

gender hierarchy 21, 22, 23–8
Gissing, George 125–6
Greenslade, W. 129
Grey, Earl 33
Grimm, Jacob 42
guilt, *Tess of the d'Urbervilles* 131–
    2, 133, 140

Hall, C. 155
Hard Times (Dickens) 34
Hardy, Thomas
    'The Dorsetshire Labourer' 137
    social change 141
    Tess of the d'Urbervilles 121,
        123–43
Heller, D. 78
Herbert, George 122–3
hermeneutic codes 5
Hirsch, P. 77
Hogg, James 93, 106, 116
Hutton, R. H. 124

identity
    Bleak House 99–103, 115
    Daniel Deronda 67–9
    Little Dorrit 151
    Tess of the d'Urbervilles 130–1,
        135, 138
ideology 6–8, 163–4
imperialism
    Daniel Deronda 74–6, 88
    Vanity Fair 29–33
impurity 124–6
intention 65, 87
irony 21

Jane Eyre (Brontë) 99, 101
Jewsbury, Geraldine 25, 101, 110
Johnson, Samuel 66
Judaism 63, 74, 76–8, 80–1, 85–
    6, 89

Kaufmann, David 63
King Lear (Shakespeare) 147
Kranidis 89

Leavis, F. R. 63
linear narrative structure 147–9,
    153
Linehan, K. B. 74, 76
Little Dorrit (Dickens) 9, 10–11,
    104, 114
    character and relationships 155–
        60
    femininity 154–5
    narrative structure 147–54,
        160–1
    negatives 122, 144–7, 161–2
'Love Song of J. Alfred Prufrock,
    The' (Eliot) 16–18
Lyell, Charles 42, 43
Lyons, J. 11, 67, 94

Magdalenism (Tait) 136
magic future 67, 70, 74, 80, 85–7
Marian Withers (Jewsbury) 101,
    110
'Marion' (Tennyson) 123, 124
marriage, incest taboo 140–1, 155
Martin, C. A. 76–7
Martineau, Harriet 22, 27
Marvell, Andrew 66
Marx, Karl 6
Mary Barton (Gaskell) 22, 110
masculinity
    Little Dorrit 153
    The Mill on the Floss 57–61
    Vanity Fair 31
metaphors, *The Mill on the Floss*
    54–5
Middlemarch (Eliot) 71, 84
Mill on the Floss, The (Eliot) 9, 39–
    40

childhood 48–50
femininity and masculinity 57–
61
flood 42
language 55–7
metaphors 54–5
moral rules 53–4
present tense 43–8
society and individual 50
suitors 50–3
Miller, A. 35, 36
Miller, Nancy K. 94
modality 9, 163
Moonstone, The (Collins) 97–8, 99
morality
The Mill on the Floss 53–4
Tess of the d'Urbervilles 127–8
Morris, William 41
Müller, Max 108

narrative
chronotopes 8
questions 15–16
narrative structure, *Little Dorrit*
147–54
narrators 95, 163
Bleak House 93, 96–9, 106–11,
114–15, 116–17
Vanity Fair 19–21, 93
natural history 45
nature, *Tess of the d'Urbervilles*
128–30
Nead, L. 3
negatives 9, 10–11, 121–4
Freud 149–50
Little Dorrit 144–7, 154, 161–2
Tess of the d'Urbervilles 123–5,
127–8, 130, 134, 135, 139
Newton, Judith 22, 23, 24
Nightingale, Florence 101, 103,
105, 106, 161

non-compliant negatives 121, 146
non-existence 121, 146
North and South (Gaskell) 23, 110
Norton, S. M. 26

'Ode on the Intimations of
Immortality from Recollec-
tions of Early Childhood'
(Wordsworth) 49–50
Oliphant, Margaret 139–40
omne-narrator 96–9, 106–11,
115, 116–17
Origin of Species, The (Darwin) 42,
47, 96
Our Mutual Friend (Dickens)
153–4

paradise 48
Passage to India, A (Forster) 95
past 40–2
Bleak House 102
Daniel Deronda 69–70, 71
The Mill on the Floss 52
performance 4
posing questions 17
poverty 137–8
power relations
Bleak House 115
Daniel Deronda 74–6, 89
Vanity Fair 21–34
Praeterita (Ruskin) 94
Pratt, M. L. 9
prediction 65, 83
present 39, 40–2
Bleak House 95, 106, 109
Daniel Deronda 81
The Mill on the Floss 43–9
*Private Memoirs and Confessions of
a Justified Sinner, The* (Hogg)
93, 106, 116
proaretic codes 5

Prostitution (Acton) 136
purity 124–5

questions 9, 15–16
   'Love Song of J. Alfred
      Prufrock, The' (Eliot) 16–18
   Vanity Fair 15

racism 30–32, 75–8
rank 34
rape 132–3
referential codes 5
refusal to comply 121, 146
rejection 121, 146
Ricardo, David 34
Riehl, Wilhelm Heinrich 45
Rignall, J. 55
Robinson Crusoe (Defoe) 147
Roman Charity 159, 160
'Roman Wall Blues' (Auden) 96
Ruskin, John 34, 40, 41, 57, 94
Ruth (Gaskell) 125–6

Sadoff, D. 158
sanitation 111–12
Saussure, Ferdinand de 2–3, 5–6
science 41–3
scope 1–2
   negatives 122, 146–7
seduction 132–3
self *see* identity
self-referentiality 20, 21
semantic codes 5
semic codes 5
semiology 2–3
sentence structure 1–2, 3
sexuality
   Bleak House 103–4, 106
   Little Dorrit 157–60
   and social class 136
   Tess of the d'Urbervilles 126–7,

      130
Shakespeare, William 96, 122, 147
shame 130–1, 134, 140
Shillingsburg, P. 17
Shirley (Brontë) 23, 101, 110
Showalter, E. 144
Shuttleworth, S. 94–5, 103
'Sighs and Groans' (Herbert) 122–
   3
signified 5–6
signifier 5–6
signs 2–3, 4, 5
Smith, Stanley 140
social class 21–3
   Bleak House 110–14
   Tess of the d'Urbervilles 136–7
   Vanity Fair 28–30, 34
social distortion 105–6
social unrest 28–30, 140, 141
Spenser, Edmund 65–6, 123
Squires, M. 148
Sussman, H. 58
Swinburne, Algernon 61
Sybil (Disraeli) 111, 113
symbolic codes 5
syntactic codes 5

Tait, William 136
Tale of Two Cities, A (Dickens) 40
Tennyson, Alfred, Lord 123, 124
tense 9, 39–40, 163
   see also future; past; present
Tess of the d'Urbervilles (Hardy) 9,
   10–11, 138–43
   guilt 131–2
   identity 130–1
   marriage 134–6
   morality 127–8
   murder 140
   nature 128–30
   negatives 121, 123–5

rape/seduction scene 132–3
rural poverty 136–8
sexuality 126–7
violence 141–2
Thackeray, William Makepeace
    28, 29, 30
    Vanity Fair 15, 18–36
Thomas à Kempis 51, 56
time 8, 95–6, 107, 108
'To His Coy Mistress' (Marvell) 66
Todorov, T. 5
Traugott, E. C. 9
Trilling, Lionel 147, 154
Tristan, Flora 112
truth 96

Unclassed, The (Gissing) 125–6
United States, Civil War 71–2

Vanity Fair (Thackeray) 9, 15
    Amelia–Becky pairing 23–7
    commodification 34–6
    imperialism 30–34
    narrative monologue 19–21
    narrator 93

power relations 21–3
questions 18–19
social unrest 28–30
verbal codes 5
Villette (Brontë) 103

Walkowitz, J. 136
witnesses 98
Wittgenstein, Ludwig 15, 19, 93,
    94, 121
women
    as cult-figure 147
    Daniel Deronda 79
    gender hierarchy 21, 22
    identity 100–1
    purity 124
    Vanity Fair 22–4
    see also femininity
Wordsworth, William 49–50
worthlessness 134, 139

x-questions 17, 18–19, 23

yes/no questions 17